Dying without Fear

Dr. Paul Chaloux

DYING
WITHOUT
FEAR

SOPHIA INSTITUTE PRESS
Manchester, New Hampshire

Nihil obstat: Very Rev. Francis de Rosa, *Censor Deputatus*
Imprimatur: + Michael F. Burbidge, Bishop of Arlington
March 20, 2023

Sophia Institute Press
Box 5284, Manchester, NH 03108
1-800-888-9344
www.SophiaInstitute.com

Sophia Institute Press is a registered trademark of Sophia Institute.

paperback ISBN 978-1-64413-868-7

ebook ISBN 978-1-64413-869-4

Library of Congress Control Number: 2023936982

2nd printing

To my mother, Dolores (Dolly) Chaloux,
who inspired this book,
and to my wife, Sue,
who made it possible

Contents

Acknowledgments ix

Section I
The Theology of Suffering and Death

1. Introduction 3

2. Revisiting the Nature and Power of God 9

3. Understanding Our Role in God's Plan 35

4. God Uses Evil and Suffering to Bring about
   Greater Good. 43

5. Suffering and Its Four Tasks 53

6. Rethinking Dying and Terminal Suffering 65

7. Rethinking Death. 93

8. Particular Judgment, Heaven, Hell, and Purgatory 103

9. The Last Day 109

Section II
Dying with Grace

10. What Kills Us. 119

11. Choices for Treatment 129

12. Living Well with a Terminal Disease 145

13. Planning for Life after Death 159

Section III
Dealing with the Dying
and Death of Loved Ones

14. The Suicide of a Loved One 169

15. The Unexpected Death of a Loved One 175

16. The Five Needs of the Terminally Ill 179

17. Choosing a Living Environment
    for a Dying Loved One 185

18. Why Did My Innocent Child Die? 193

19. Why Did My Parent Die When I Was Young? 199

20. Why Did My Spouse Die? 205

21. Coping with Parental Death as an Adult. 215

22. Embracing Joy in Suffering and Death 217

    Discussion Questions. 221

    About the Author .227

Acknowledgments

I want to acknowledge that Sue Chaloux, Rich Chaloux, Janet Baum, Tom A. Chaloux, Karen Boucher Romano, Marcel Chaloux, Lorraine Fontaine, Jim Ball, Sr. Mary Catherine Blanding, Allison Brown, Jenny Echevarria, Garrett Johnson, and Colleen Lang critiqued and contributed insight to the original draft of this book. Thank you for your aid in making this the best it could be.

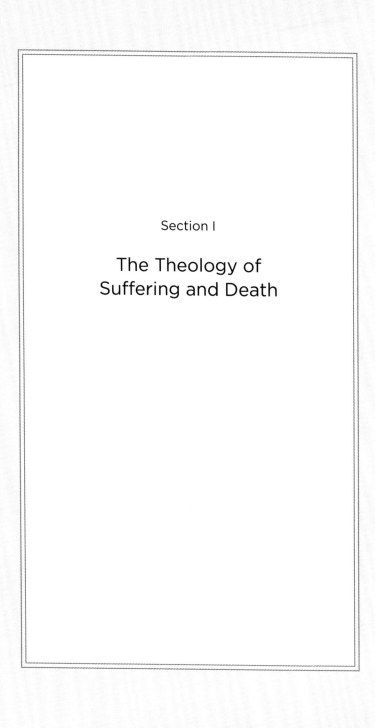

Section I

The Theology of Suffering and Death

Chapter 1

Introduction

Everyone suffers in life, and everyone dies. People who read a book on suffering and death are not questioning that, nor are they questioning the existence of God. True atheists would never search for the meaning behind suffering and death, because for there to be meaning behind these experiences, then there would need to be a plan and a planner, which would mean a god. What a suffering or dying person wants to know is why this is happening at this particular time and in this particular manner and what is going to happen next. Many people suffering from a terminal injury or illness, or witnessing the loss of a loved one, will wonder whether God is punishing them or has abandoned them in their time of need. Although suffering and death are theologically the result of the grave moral evil that was our first parents' rebellion against God's will (the "Fall of Man"), this book will show definitively that suffering and death can be used by a loving and merciful God to bring us to eternal joy.

The theology offered here is consistent with the doctrine of the Catholic Church, which is very important to me because I do not want to lead anyone into error. Much of it was validated when my first book, *Why All People Suffer*, was given the *nihil obstat* and bishop's *imprimatur* after investigation by the Most Rev. Michael Burbidge, bishop of Arlington, Virginia. This book received the same validations. In addition, I have done my best to obtain all the critical thoughts from the most impeccable Catholic sources: Sacred Scripture, the *Catechism of the Catholic Church*, St. Thomas Aquinas's *Summa Theologiae*, and St. John Paul II's *Salvifici Doloris*. I've cited these throughout the book, to demonstrate that the theology used in this book is completely consistent with existing Catholic doctrine.

That said, for those that want to read this book as a pastoral guide to death and dying and not as a full theology, you can skip ahead to chapter 6 after the introduction and find what you need. The second section of the book focuses on how to interpret this theology and use it when you are terminally injured or terminally ill to prioritize how you spend your remaining time, energy, and resources to die well. The third section of the book is for caregivers and discusses how to properly care for the dying and how to come to understand a loved one's death in God's plan. You will note that I make ample use of my own family history to explain these points. This serves not only to illustrate the points but also to help the reader understand the genesis of this book. Also at the end of the book is a set of discussion questions for each chapter for readers to consider.

This book is the culmination of an amazing journey, one that I neither planned nor anticipated yet felt strangely compelled to take. In fact, I feel like I was being driven to it by circumstances largely outside my control, with numerous people contributing to it, seemingly unwittingly. The journey seemed to begin with a very vivid dream in May 2013; but in retrospect, the seeds had been planted long before that.

In May 2013, my oldest daughter, Kathy, graduated from Cornell University, and I was impressed by one of her professors, who had given up a lucrative job in her industry to go back to school and teach the next generation. At the time, I was in a similar situation, having worked for one of the great American corporations for over thirty years, the last decade of which was spent planning the manufacturing strategy for its most capital-intensive division. I was unhappy in my job, however, for a variety of reasons. The most significant of these reasons was that the company had decided to divest itself of the division that I had spent my whole career building up. In a way, it was not surprising that, following that graduation, I had a vivid dream telling me that I, too, should give up my lucrative position and go back to school and teach. There was a twist, however: it would not be to teach what I had learned in my professional life.

Back in the summer of 2000, I had experienced a life-changing sequence of events that began with a sacramental Confession. I no longer remember the sins I confessed, but I do remember the penance: attend an optional weekday Mass. Although I was a conscientious Sunday communicant, I had never attended a weekday Mass, and for some reason I felt a trepidation to do so. I hesitated for a few days, but I felt compelled to go because I'd told the priest that I would. I finally went, and it felt profoundly right to me, so right that I continue to attend daily Mass to this day. A few months later, when my daughter Kathy was about to enter the fourth grade, the parish put out a call for catechists. I volunteered.

I had never taught anything before, but teaching came naturally to me. I was astonished, however, by how little I actually knew about the Faith, despite having read the Bible daily since the sixth grade, which represented a period of about twenty-five years by that time. In truth, I had never even prayed the Rosary. I found myself learning from the textbook, just like the students did.

I embarked on a program to correct that deficiency, reading voraciously on Church doctrine, the lives of the saints, and even engaging in online apologetics. I became a more effective catechist, and two years later, I took on a second weekly class, in part so that I could also teach my three sons. Some years later Sister Marie Pappas, who also happened to host "*Pathways to Learning*," a weekly nationwide show on SiriusXM satellite radio, took over the school of religion in our parish and began encouraging me to expand my catechetical reach beyond the parish. It was her voice that I heard in the dream telling me to become a teacher of teachers, but in the field of catechetics. The dream itself was vivid and strangely compelling, not that I can remember anything about it other than the message to quit my job, get a doctorate, and teach the teachers. I talked it over with my wife, Sue, and she was very supportive, so I pursued it with vigor.

Through a series of improbable events described later in the book, over the next eight years, I earned a master's degree in religious education from Fordham University, a Ph.D. in Moral Theology and Ethics from the Catholic University of America, wrote *Why All People Suffer* and promoted it with a couple of dozen live radio and TV interviews, ten articles on *Catholic Exchange*, and both a book and an author website. I also taught at three levels: as a catechist at my local parish, as an adjunct professor at Catholic University and as a featured lecturer on suffering at the Avila Institute for Spiritual Direction.

I am writing this particular book because terminal suffering is a huge challenge for people, and I understand dying much better than I did when I wrote *Why All People Suffer*. This understanding came from insights from my students at the Avila Institute, several of whom worked with the dying, coupled with my own degradation from Parkinson's Disease and the death of my mother, Dolores

(Dolly) Chaloux on May 8, 2022 (fittingly on Mother's Day) after a long battle with dementia.

Writing these two books, was unexpected but cathartic to do, as I contemplated my life journey and studied what the Church has to say about it. What I found out gave me solace in my suffering and the courage to face the real possibility of death without fear. My belief is that what I learned is truth and will benefit others, so I am sharing it through these two books, which are grounded in Church teaching, my own experiences, and those of immediate family members going back three generations.

I am not sure where this will lead or who will benefit. I now know that that is out of my hands and to just trust in God, who has led me this far. I am happy and blessed to have this role, whatever it turns out to be. Suffering has a way of turning a person inward, toward where God resides. I know that God takes no delight in human discomfort, but I see now that it is unavoidable when breaking humans of the vices with which we have become comfortable, in order to set us firmly on the path of redemption. I also have come to understand that God must truly love us if He puts this much effort into keeping us on the path to joy. This is, after all, the same God who waits anxiously for the Prodigal Son to return (Luke 15:11–32). I say to all who may happen to read this: God has a plan for you and even if you cannot see where it is going, trust Him and follow where He leads you. It will be a remarkable journey and you will not regret it.

Chapter 2

Revisiting the Nature and Power of God

Questions about God

Understanding the meaning and purpose of suffering and death in God's plan requires first understanding the nature and power of God and His relationship with man. Most people do not have a good understanding of the nature and power of God and tend to severely underestimate the Creator of all that exists, some to the point of denying that God even exists.

One such person was the ancient Greek philosopher Epicurus, who explained in the fourth century before Christ that he could not reconcile the existence of evil in the world with a good and all-powerful God. He reasoned that suffering was an evil that opposed God's goodness and must be removed. He further notes that since there is suffering in the world, God was either not powerful enough to stop it or did not want to stop it because He was either indifferent to His creation or He was actually malicious, wanting the people to suffer for sadistic reasons. In the end, Epicurus felt that if there was a God, He would be all powerful and good and would destroy the evil and suffering that opposed His goodness;

so in the presence of evil, Epicurus concluded that there was no God.[1]

Since the "Enlightenment" in the seventeenth century, modern man has claimed increasing power for himself while giving God less and less credit. Forty years ago, in 1981, Rabbi Harold S. Kushner wrote the highly acclaimed and very popular book *When Bad Things Happen to Good People* in response to the death of his 14-year-old son Aaron, a victim of progeria, a genetic disorder that causes accelerated aging, resulting in death before age twenty. Aaron's sickness and death were understandably devastating to Kushner and his family and as he poignantly describes, it caused him to reevaluate his view of God as the all-good and all-powerful Creator of the universe. The way Kushner describes his dilemma is to take three statements which he believes sums up the situation, using the book of Job as his basis:

- God is all-powerful and causes everything that happens in the world. Nothing happens without God willing it.
- God is just and fair and stands for people getting what they deserve, so that the good prosper and the wicked are punished.
- Job is a good person.[2]

Kushner has a problem because he can't see any way that all three conditions can be simultaneously met in situations like his, where his son is suffering so intensely. This is not a new problem. This is the same dilemma posed by Epicurus over two millennia earlier.

---

[1] David Konstan, "Epicurus," *The Stanford Encyclopedia of Philosophy*, Summer 2018 edition, ed. Edward N. Zalta, https://plato.stanford. edu/archives/sum2018/entries/epicurus/.

[2] Harold S. Kushner, *When Bad Things Happen to Good People* (New York: Avon Books, 1981), 37.

Since then, millions of other people, when confronted with evil and suffering in their lives, have come to the same conclusion as Epicurus: that there is no God. However, Rabbi Kushner was not willing to give up his view that God exists, and that God is just. Nor was he willing to concede that he or his son had done anything to deserve punishment: they were good people. That left the good Rabbi with seemingly one solution to solve the dilemma: to deny that God was all-powerful. Kushner offered up a God who could create a universe but has no power to alter it after the fact other than to provide strength, hope and courage in times of need.[3] This solution was perfect for the general attitude of 1980's society because it preserved the vision of a loving God while removing any responsibility for anything that was onerous from Him by creating a concept of fate to which even God is subservient.

Rabbi Kushner sold over four million copies of *When Bad Things Happen to Good People*, not because it was true, but because many people desired it to be true. This is not to say that the Rabbi and his millions of like-minded followers had it all wrong – their instinctive views that God is just, and that suffering is not always or even usually a sign of the guilt of the sufferer were correct as shown in the Book of Job. The Rabbi's solution to the problem of evil has great appeal to those who feel guilty because they see suffering as a punishment for evils they committed or who were angry at God for punishing them unjustly. To find a solution that eliminated the feelings of guilt and anger was freeing and the fact that the solution required an impoverished God was actually a benefit for his target audience. In fact, a supportive, yet largely ineffective God was perfect for the humanists of modern society,

---

[3] Ibid., 43–45.

who had been arguing against the power of God and worshiping the secular successes of mankind for centuries.

No matter how comforting it might be, Kushner's solution simply does not ring true to Christians and others who recognize that God is indeed all powerful and that He definitely has healing powers, as demonstrated multiple times by Jesus Christ.[4] The problem for Rabbi Kushner and also for Epicurus is they do not recognize that their values are not aligned with God, so they judge justice based on a completely different standard.

The obvious answer to the dilemma lies not with the diminishment or outright denial of God, the Creator and sustainer of the universe; it lies in correctly understanding God's goals for humanity and how evil, suffering, and death fit into His plans to meet those goals. This is because the truth, which is a statement of reality, is logically the same from all perspectives and must be always consistent with all other truths. If an all-powerful loving God exists and so do evil, suffering, and death, it stands to reason that they must serve God's interests in some way, or He would have destroyed them.

God's Goals for Humanity

God made man in His image so that man could eventually become like Him and share in His life of eternal joy. As St. Catherine of Siena said, "Everything comes from love, all is ordained for the salvation of man, God does nothing without this goal in mind" (CCC 313). This is the key to understanding the problem of evil. God has much greater expectations for man than what we have

---

[4] There are sixteen references to Jesus healing in Matthew's Gospel alone, including 8:5-13 (the centurion's servant); 8:14-15 (Peter's mother-in-law); 8:16-17 (townspeople); 9:1-8 (a paralytic).

experienced on earth; therefore, it is a sign of His love and mercy that He uses evil, suffering, and death to lead us to share in His divine nature and to live with Him forever in joy and happiness. What we perceive as detrimental to us in the short term is actually medicinal in the long term.

Once it is clear that God is both just and all-powerful and desires the salvation of humanity, then the obvious solution to the problem of evil is that God must be able to use evil and suffering to bring about the salvation of man, which in turn transforms death into the gateway to eternal life. In fairness to both Kushner and Epicurus, this solution is made much more obvious for Christians because of the role the suffering of Jesus has in our redemption and the fact that His Resurrection proved there is life after death. Neither Kushner's nor Epicurus's theologies consider the concept of an afterlife or the need for human salvation or redemption.[5] Kushner's view is that since we cannot know for certain that there is an afterlife, we should presume that it does not exist and look for meaning and justice in this world.[6] Unfortunately, this assumption is self-limiting and does not consider that an all-powerful God can bring good from evil (CCC 412).

In the end, bad things do not happen only to good people. Indeed, all people suffer. This is not, as Rabbi Kushner presumed forty years ago, because of God's inability to help us. It is a loving God helping us to become like Him, directing, protecting, and perfecting us through the four tasks of suffering so we can live with Him in eternal joy. The truth is that the all-powerful God uses suffering to lead us to a life of abundance, and once we

---

[5] Kushner, *Bad Things*, 28-29; Konstan, "Epicurus."
[6] Kushner, *Bad Things*, 29.

understand that, we can have true joy, not just the peace of mind that was satisfying to audiences forty years ago.

It is not all that surprising that Rabbi Kushner and Epicurus, given their backgrounds, could not make this connection. They were working from a flawed theological base that precluded them from arriving at the correct answer. The fact that neither man could answer the most basic questions with solutions that would not require them to compromise known truths is a clear indication that at least a subset of their assumptions or logic is wrong.[7] To be fair to both men, neither Kushner nor Epicurus could grasp the concept of redemptive suffering because neither of them believed in an afterlife, and without that, there is no redemption.[8] Redemptive suffering is, however, a central tenet of Catholicism and Christianity in general because it is Christ's sacrifice on the Cross that redeemed humanity. As Jesus Himself proclaimed at the Last Supper, words repeated in every Mass in the Eucharistic Prayer, "This is my blood of the covenant, which will be shed on behalf of many for the forgiveness of sins" (Matt. 26:28).

If Rabbi Kushner and Epicurus had the accumulated theological knowledge of the Catholic Church to rely upon in formulating their solutions, their path to understanding the meaning of suffering and death would have been immeasurably easier. This is not to say that Catholics easily grasp the roles of evil, suffering, and death in God's plan. It merely points out that the theological

---

[7] Kushner could not answer why his son died, defaulting to the non-answer that it was fate and that the all-powerful God is powerless to stop it. Epicurus could not answer why a good and all-powerful God could allow evil and suffering to exist, defaulting to a position that there is no God.

[8] Kushner, *Bad Things*, 28–29; Konstan, "Epicurus."

base developed by the Church is robust and consistent with a point of view that God not only coexists with evil, suffering, and death but uses them productively to carry out His plan for the world (CCC 312). After all, the suffering and death of Jesus Christ, which brought about the salvation of man, is the defining event of Christianity through which God's mercy and love show themselves most brightly. This perspective changes everything in how we view suffering, death, and, in fact, God and ourselves.

The Power of God

Those who doubt the power or existence of God would do well to consider God's response to Moses when they met at the burning bush on Mount Horeb and Moses asked His name. He answers, "I am who I am" and adds, "This is my title for all generations" (Exod. 3:14–15). In saying this, He is stating that He not only exists but is the source of all that exists.

St. Thomas Aquinas weighs in on this, saying, "God brought things into being in order that His goodness might be communicated to creatures and, at the same time, represented by them; and because His goodness could not be adequately represented by one creature alone, He produced many and diverse creatures, that what was wanting to one in the representation of the divine goodness might be supplied by another."[9] So, to extend St. Thomas's thoughts a little further, he is saying that God is greater than the sum of His creatures. No wonder we cannot see God directly. It would be like a microbe trying to see a human, only with an even greater differential. We just do not have an aperture wide enough to capture God all at once, even if we had the ability to sense the spiritual world. The best we can do to get a sense of His greatness

---

[9] *Summa Theologiae* [hereafter cited as *ST*] I, q. 47, art. 1.

is to contemplate what we have seen of His works: the diversity and number of His creatures or, maybe even more powerfully, by gazing into the nighttime sky and contemplating the vastness of the universe before us.

Finally, there is no power in the universe that can seriously oppose God. God's power dwarfs that of Satan, who has great power as a purely spiritual being but not nearly enough to prevent the building up of God's Kingdom (CCC 395). The only time Satan directly confronts Jesus in Scripture, Jesus humors him briefly—as Satan tries his best to tempt Jesus with food, power, and wealth—and then dismisses him with the words "Get away, Satan." Satan follows this command and leaves without another word (Matt. 4:1-10). In a similar way, the lesser demons are ordered out of people by Jesus throughout the four Gospel accounts, and all of them immediately comply without pushback (Matt. 8:28-34; 9:32-34; 12:22-32; Mark 9:14-29; 7:26-30; Luke 8:26-39).

God made Satan. And, like all creation, Satan only exists by the will of God, and God knows what motivates him (CCC 301). Further, with His foresight, God knows every move Satan will make before he makes it, so He can easily counter to use Satan's malice to bring about good. There are no surprises and no unimportant situations with an all-powerful God who has perfect foresight.

Probably the greatest show of God's power and superior intelligence involves Satan and the Crucifixion. Satan was successful in convincing Eve to eat the fruit from the tree of knowledge of good and evil despite God's commandment (Gen. 3:2-4). God, with perfect foresight, undoubtedly anticipated this because He had the plan in motion to save humanity and bring it home through the Crucifixion and Resurrection of His Son, Jesus Christ. For this plan to work, He needed Jesus to be publicly executed so that there could be no doubt of His death when He was resurrected.

So who better to make it painful and showy than Satan. God used Satan's malice against him, knowing that Satan could not resist the chance to exploit the weakness of one of Jesus' apostles to get at Jesus and, through him, attack God. Judas showed such a weakness at the anointing of Jesus by Mary, the sister of Lazarus, when Judas was rebuked by Jesus for complaining that Mary had "wasted" the valuable perfume that could have been sold to produce money to give to the poor (John 12:1-7). No doubt stung by the rebuke, and perhaps aware that some of the other apostles knew he was stealing from the common funds he held (which John confirms in his Gospel in John 12:6), Judas then visited the chief priests the first day back in Jerusalem and offered to turn Jesus over to them (Mark 14:10-11; Luke 22:3-4).

Seizing the opportunity, as God foresaw, Satan entered Judas at the Last Supper and made the arrangements necessary to turn Jesus over to be crucified (John 13:27). You can just imagine how gleeful Satan probably was as the Jews and Romans collaborated in turning away from the Son of God and killed Him in a gruesome public spectacle. That glee probably turned into bitter frustration three days later when Satan realized he had played a big part in God's plan leading to the redemption of humanity, which Satan hates.

Additionally, the power of God to create is far beyond anything else we have witnessed. God can create anything He wants from nothing using only His word. This was made clear in Genesis 1, where God made everything and everything He made was good for its intended purpose.

God's Foresight and Direction

Probably the most underappreciated aspect of God's capabilities is His foresight. Because God exists outside of time, He sees past, present, and future at once. To understand how this works in theory, imagine you are the author of a book on the life of a character. Because you're outside the book, you can turn to any page of the book at any time and see where the character is in his life, without affecting the character. Since you're the author of the book, if you find that something needs changing, you are free to do that. God is the author of the universe but is outside it, so He can do the same. This allows Him to see the effects of people's actions before they actually make their choices. If He does not like the outcome, He will change the circumstances so that our personal tendencies will be aligned with what He desires to be done, while at the same time He anticipates our next moves and compensates for them to make His global plan work. God can do this without disrupting human free will by adjusting the environment in a way that makes His desired outcome the natural choice for the people involved.

I have experienced this in a most obvious way in my own life. When I first had the dream about "teaching the teachers" that I described in the introduction of this book, there were a number of impediments that God knew would have kept me from saying yes. The first was my worry about negatively affecting my family to follow a dream. This concern disappeared quickly, as my wife, Sue, was fully supportive of me following my dream from the be-ginning—it also didn't hurt that her new job could be done from anywhere. Further, my two oldest children, Kathy and Tom, who had graduated from college, were moving out on their own, and the two youngest, John and Dan, would be away at college anyway. The second potential impediment was that I loved playing and coaching sports; I would have had a tough time giving them up if Parkinson's disease had not made me completely uncompetitive. The third was my loyalty to my job and the community it served, but the company sold my division, leaving me with nothing to do about it. With those significant impediments removed, doing God's will for me became clear, and the natural and freely made choice was to say yes. This gave me new appreciation for Jesus' claim in St. Matthew's Gospel that His yoke is easy and His burden light (Matt. 11:28-30). This kind of thing happened multiple times for me in the course of a few years, so I was able to pick up the pattern. Again, this was part of His plan for my education. In retrospect, I can see that some of these circumstances were set up years in advance, and the creativity and nuance in the progression are extremely impressive. There simply is no way I could have done this on my own, as you will see.

My initial thoughts after the pivotal dream were that I was going to move to Boston and study religious education at Boston College, with the goal of teaching future directors of religious education (DREs) how to teach morality in their CCD (religious education) programs, and to regularly attend Red Sox games at Fenway Park. Sue loves Boston so she was "all in" with this plan. That God's plan for me was so far superior to my own expectations was not clear at that point. That understanding came in stages. In my experience, He provides exactly what we need, exactly when we need it, so we do exactly what is needed from us with nothing wasted. God is amazingly efficient in this, as you might expect from a perfect being.

The first thing He needed for me to do for His plan was to get me to go to Catholic University in D.C. He did this by making my credentials more appealing to Catholic than they were to Boston College so that only Catholic accepted my application. I have no idea what made the difference, and it really does not matter. He reinforced this by giving me the opportunity to interview live at Catholic, which I fully enjoyed, leaving me with a very positive view of the place, the students, the faculty, and the programs I was to pursue. I knew with all my being that I was in the right place and told Sue that I was hoping Boston College would turn me down, which, as it turned out, they did shortly afterward.

It was at this time that God started to reveal the next part of my education, but I was completely blind to what was happening because it represented a radical departure from my own plans. My mother, who was eighty-three years old at that time, had been living with my sister Maria in her home in Aldie, Virginia, since my father had passed away four years earlier. My brother Richard, who had selflessly moved in with both parents to help care for them in their home four years previously, also moved in with them in Maria's home. Maria wanted to move to the Boston suburbs for personal reasons, but that would have been difficult to do without finding living arrangements for my mother. I discussed the situation with Sue, and she suggested that the obvious solution was to buy a house in Washington big enough to accommodate both Rich and my mom, freeing up Maria to move. We discussed it with the other family members and subsequently purchased a home in Arlington, Virginia, with Rich and had a first-floor suite built for my mother.

This had two big effects on me. First, it gave me firsthand experience in caring for an elder loved one, and second, it locked me into pursuing the dream when I was diagnosed with Parkinson's disease a few days later. I had no idea at the time why this was important because I had no thoughts at the time of pursuing anything related to suffering. God used my new neurologist for that purpose, which was quite surprising. Obviously, He had prompted some of her patients to ask her why they were suffering in a memorable enough way that, when presented with a doctoral theology student, she felt compelled to ask me the question that set all of this activity off: "Why do people suffer?" It was not the kind of question I was expecting, and since I had never considered it and it was not my field of study, I had no answer for her. She was adamant that I should be studying it, because as she explained, "Everyone asks doctors this every day, and we never have an answer for them." I was noncommittal, but the seed had been planted and I couldn't get it out of my mind.

Now that God had tweaked my interest in suffering, the next thing to arrange was for me to get the necessary learning to pursue this interest in a credible way. First on the agenda was to train me to write prose and to conduct and document academic research to the level required at a research university like Catholic, skills not highly developed in engineering programs or in corporate America. Because I was the only Ph.D. catechetical candidate at Catholic in my cohort, I was given an independent study class with Fr. Emanuel Magro, a priest from Malta who had worked at the Library of Congress to put himself through the Ph.D. program several years earlier. Fr. Magro was an excellent mentor, assigning me weekly research papers that he would go through in intimate detail with me, pointing out ways to improve my writing and to document my sources efficiently and accurately. This was exactly the one-on-one attention I needed in my first in-person class in over thirty years.

Next on the agenda was to prove to me that suffering was a better topic for me than developing a curriculum for teaching moral theology. This initial intention worked out for me because, although my major was catechetics, I was minoring in moral theology and ethics, so I took classes in each. In my second semester, there was an ethics class offered, Social and Spiritual Practices in Moral Formation, that seemed to fit my needs perfectly. It did at that, but not in the way I thought it would. Instead of writing about my planned dissertation topic on teaching moral theology to youth and young adults, which would have fit perfectly in this class, I felt compelled to write "Suffering as a Catalyst for Conversion." With this thirty-three-page paper, I developed the basic theology that led to my doctoral dissertation, to my first book, and now to this offering. In doing so, I became convinced that this was my true calling and got the attention of the professor, Dr. Paul Scherz, who told me that the topic had merit as a dissertation topic and that he would be happy to direct it, if I should choose to pursue it. This was important because Dr. Scherz is exceptionally diligent, knowledgeable, and responsive, essential qualities in a good director, and good directors are highly in demand and hard to get.

The next step necessary to make the plan work was that I had to be in the moral theology department to pursue a dissertation on suffering. Remember that by mutual agreement, when I entered the university, I joined the catechetics department, which as I described above was critical to my development. Now I needed to transfer to moral theology to make the plan work, so I petitioned the acting dean to allow me to dual major in moral theology and catechetics. They told me my plan was unworkable but that they had a better solution. The current head of the catechetics department was leaving the university for personal reasons, and until they replaced her, they had no one they felt was qualified to direct my dissertation. Furthermore, based on my work in the three moral theology classes I had taken, they wanted me to transfer to moral theology for my dissertation. I was dumbfounded. Just a year before, I had been turned down by every moral theology department I had applied to—and deservedly so, because, as I now understood, I lacked the prerequisites. Nevertheless, in God's hands, what I had been perceiving as a problem became no problem at all.

This kind of subtle direction has continued right to the present. I had a chance encounter with Michael Warsaw, chairman and CEO of EWTN, the largest Catholic media company in the world, at a scholarship dinner in December 2018. He convinced me that the project had merit and encouraged me to publish it for general audiences. His kind words of encouragement motivated me to press forward on the project when things were less than perfect. Interestingly, I thought for sure that the chance encounter with Mr. Warsaw meant he was going to publish the book, but I was never able to contact him again. Perhaps all I was supposed to get out of that meeting was the encouragement to pursue a book on suffering for general audiences. That sustained me through the publisher search, and I was blessed to end up at Sophia Press, a small but very reputable Catholic publisher. Their staff is excellent, and they were patient with me as I learned how to navigate the world of publishing and marketing a book. Never did I anticipate being asked to weigh in on difficult theological questions on the nature of evil, God, suffering, and death on national television. But I found myself well prepared to do so, giving credence to the Catholic mantra that God gives us what we need for the roles that He has in mind for us.

God's Management Skills

This deft directing of my life, which still allows me total free will, highlights how impressive God's project management skills truly are. Imagine managing an entire universe over thousands of years, including individually planning every moment and interaction of billions of humans on earth, at the level He is managing me, arranging for the right people with the right message to come into my life at the right time. Their impact often came without their knowledge that they did anything special, because for them, they were only doing what came naturally given the circumstances that were presented to them. Jesus confirms the detailed level God works at, telling us that God notices every sparrow and even the hairs on our heads are counted (Luke 12:7).

In addition, God is amazingly efficient and focused on our salvation, with the same event influencing multiple people in multiple ways. For example, natural disasters like floods, hurricanes, and blizzards affect thousands of people, touching each in their own individual ways and each for the salvation of souls. Some will lose possessions that have distracted them from doing the things they need to do for their salvation. Others will take the opportunity to help their neighbors while a few will do the opposite, taking advantage of their weakness. Even in these cases, if their victims lovingly show them the reality of what they have done and the perpetrator repents, it can work toward salvation.

Seeing God

Any thoughts of a diminished God are inconsistent with the facts as we know them. It is not surprising that we cannot physically see God prior to death, because He is, in the words of the *Catechism*, "greater than all His works" and possesses greatness that is "unsearchable" (CCC 300). We simply do not have the sensory capability to perceive Him directly. We can see, however, the fruits of His works, each of which tells us something about the nature of God and, in total, shows His awesome power. We see He has great imagination and a love of diversity, from the diversity of men, of creatures, and of landscapes we observe. He plans at the universal level, and yet His attention to detail is exquisite, being built up from the subatomic level. Who has not marveled at the beauty of the night sky and also at the beauty of a single snowflake?

Those who do not believe are quick to point out that there is no physical evidence God exists, and in doing so they disregard the fruits of His work that include themselves and everything their eyes can see, their ears can hear, or their hands can touch. We should note the inconsistency in the argument, because they cannot see the air they breathe either, but they do not doubt it exists, because of the work that it does. They understand that if they do not have air to breathe, they will die. Everyone is confident about this because they can do a simple experiment to test it by holding their breath, shutting the lungs off from the air, simulating what it would be like if there were no air. To exist, we need God more than air, but there is no equivalent test to prove it, because even if we seek to shut ourselves off from God, He does not abandon us.

Humans learn things by relating new ideas to ones we've previously experienced through the five senses (hearing, sight, touch, smell, and taste). It is very difficult to explain something to someone who has no relevant experience or, worse, lacks the sensory capability to detect it. For instance, how would you explain the concept of "yellow" to a man born blind? We struggle to describe God or even assess His existence because we lack the ability to sense a spiritual being, and He is so far superior to anything else that we have no truly relevant basis to use as a comparison. When we describe Him with human characteristics, we are severely underestimating Him, but in many cases, that is the best way we can communicate His being in a manner that can be understood by other humans. God obviously understands this as well and reaches out to reveal Himself to us when it suits His purposes. Sometimes this is done by granting certain individuals limited ability to sense the spiritual world, like the visionaries at Lourdes and Fatima.[10]

---

[10] At Lourdes, the visionary St. Bernadette Soubirous saw the Blessed Virgin Mary eighteen times in 1858, drawing large crowds to witness the visions and ultimately leaving a spring that has had over

Other times, He brings awareness of His presence to us through the five senses as we get glimpses of Him through His works. Still others have felt His presence or sensed His movement in our lives as we ponder the events that we are part of.

As discussed above, God has revealed Himself through His works but most directly through His Son, Jesus Christ, who the Church says was sent for four reasons:

1. To save us by reconciling us with God through His sacrifice (CCC 457)
2. So that we might know God's love, as shown by the sacrifice of His Son (CCC 458)
3. To be our model of holiness, showing us how to live as God wants us to live (CCC 459)
4. To make us partakers of the divine nature: God became man so that men might become gods (CCC 460)

The Prodigal Son

One of the most profound teachings in the Christian tradition is Jesus' parable of the Prodigal Son (Luke 15:11–32), in which He

---

seven thousand unexplained cures and seventy confirmed miracles as declared by an independent medical board. Sanctuaire de Lourdes, https://www.lourdes-france.org/en/. At Fatima, three young shepherds, Lucia dos Santos, Francisco Marto, and Jacinta Marto, saw the Angel of Peace twice in 2016 and then the Blessed Virgin Mary five times in 2017. The final vision (October 13, 2017) was accompanied by the "Miracle of the Sun," which was witnessed by seventy thousand people and reported in the secular press. Katherine Arcement, "Our Lady of Fatima: The Virgin Mary Promised Three Kids a Miracle That 70,000 Gathered to See," *Washington Post*, October 13, 2017, https://www.washingtonpost.com/news/retropolis/wp/2017/10/13/our-lady-of-fatima-the-virgin-mary-promised-three-kids-a-miracle-that-70000-gathered-to-see/.

tells us God's motivation is to reunite with us, His wayward children, and that God uses suffering as a tool to make that happen. In the story, a man has two sons, and the younger one wants to live on his own and in his own way. He brazenly asks his father to give him his inheritance while he still lives, never even thinking that doing so will deplete his father's livelihood. He thinks only of himself and his desire for independence. He gathers up his belongings and heads to a foreign city, where he quickly wastes his wealth on a life of dissipation.

Left with no means of support, he suffers from hunger, and his first response is to hire himself out to a local businessman, who puts him to work as a pig herder. Still the young man suffers because he is not making enough to sustain himself. Finally, the suffering leads him to realize that his father always had enough to feed everyone well, even the lowliest of servants.

Made desperate by his ongoing suffering, the Prodigal Son decides it is time to go home to his father. However, he is self-aware enough that he recognizes he has sinned against his father by his actions, and he is worried his father will disown him and turn him away. In hopes that he can circumvent this, he prepares a speech, humbling himself and stating that he doesn't deserve to be called his father's son but would be happy to be called his servant.

What happens next is totally shocking to the son. When the son returns, his father is waiting by the side of the road, and while the boy is still far off, his father runs to him with open arms. His father cares nothing about what his son did or did not do with the property—his only focus is that his beloved son has come back. He calls on his servants to dress his son in the finest clothes and to prepare a huge feast in his honor because "this son of mine was dead, and has come to life again; he was lost, and has been found" (Luke 15:11–32).

God Is Love

It does not take a theologian or a Bible scholar to interpret this particular parable. The father is obviously God, and we collectively are the Prodigal Son. The conclusion of the Church on the nature of God is as stated by St. John in his first epistle: "God is love" (1 John 4:8). What that means for us on a practical level is best described by Jesus in the parable of the Prodigal Son as the forgiving and merciful father, who wants nothing more than to wrap his arms around us and celebrate if we come home to him. God loves us more than we love ourselves. If you are a parent, you know the love you have for your child. God's love for you is greater than that. He literally made us and sustains us in life. Without God we would not exist or take our next breath (CCC 300). This, like our physical births, can never adequately be repaid, and yet God still gives us more. In fact, He gives every one of his creatures the skills, resources, training, and opportunities required to fulfill our part in His plan. Some parts seem bigger than others, and they are, but God only expects you to do what you were made to do: "Much will be required of the person entrusted with much" (Luke 12:48). In other words, God grades on a curve.

Although man spurned God and still spurns Him, God does not abandon us to ourselves. He not only gives us being and existence, but He also maintains it (CCC 301). As discussed in the parable, God wants His wayward progeny to return to Him, and as with the Prodigal Son in the parable, it will be suffering that will turn us back. God, who is love, wants us back, not because He needs anything but because He knows we need Him. At the same time, like the father in the parable, God understands that unless His children experience the alternatives, we will not fully appreciate what He does for us or the wisdom in the laws and moral codes that lead to happiness.

The Church

Perhaps the greatest show of God's love for us is the establishment of His Church. As we saw in the parable of the Prodigal Son (Luke 15:11-32), all God wants is for us to return to Him freely in love, and He set up His Church as both His Bride and His Body to symbolize His desire for us, making use of concepts we understand to make the relationship clear. Because men are not normally called brides, the bridal analogy may initially resonate more with women, but men also understand the requirements of being a good spouse. First and foremost is the requirement of fidelity, to be devoted wholeheartedly to one's spouse. In the Old Testament, the unfaithful Israelites who pursued other gods were likened to adulteresses repeatedly by several prophets to emphasize this point.[11] Two other attributes of a good spouse are the desire to be with one's partner and the desire to support them in all that they do. God does this for us as members of the Church, and even before that as He courts us, and He expects us to do the same toward each other and toward Him.

The bridal analogy also lends credence to the body analogy because we are told that, when married, the spouses become one body (Gen. 2:24). The Church as the Body of Christ was an insight of St. Paul that was so potent and relevant he used it in two of his epistles (1 Cor. 12:12-31; Eph. 4:1-16). As Christ's Body on earth, we are to carry out His will. Indeed, St. Paul tells us that while some were made to lead as apostles, teachers, and prophets, and were given special graces to help build up the Church, every member of

---

[11] Old Testament readings relating the unfaithful Israelites to harlots or unfaithful spouses include Jer. 3:1-10; Hos. 1:1-9; Ezek. 23:1-49; and Mic. 1:1-7.

the Church has a role in bringing about God's Kingdom. He goes on to say that all are important and necessary to the success of the enterprise, and thus, we need to be supportive of one another as we all carry out God's will (1 Cor. 12:1–31).

Who Can Be Saved?

This brings us to the obvious question about who belongs to the Catholic (universal) Church and can be saved. The Catholic Church itself recognizes that all men are called to this catholic unity of the people of God but in different ways. Some are fully incorporated into the society of the Church because, possessing the Spirit of Christ, they accept all the means of salvation given to the Church and, by the bonds of the sacraments, their profession of faith, and ecclesiastical government, are "joined in the visible structure of the Church of Christ, who rules her through the supreme pontiff and all the bishops" (CCC 837).

Others are in a less perfect union with the Church and ultimately with God's will. The Orthodox churches share so much with the Catholic Church in history, doctrine, and sacramental understanding that there is little left for them to do to attain full communion. And members of ecclesial communities whose adherents believe in Christ and have been properly baptized are put in a certain, although imperfect, union with the Church (CCC 836–838).

The Jewish faith, unlike other non-Christian religions, is already a response to God's revelation in the Old Covenant. The Jewish people anxiously wait for the Messiah to come, while Christians wait for Jesus the Messiah to come again (CCC 839–840). The plan of salvation also includes the Muslims, who acknowledge God as the Creator (CCC 841). So, although the further you get from Catholic doctrine and practice, the greater the impediments are to salvation, there remains hope for all who wish to be members of God's Kingdom and who do their best to share in the divine nature as they understand it (CCC 843-844).

It should be very clear at this stage that it is our actions toward God and each other, not our words, that matter to God. If we do not show our love of God by doing His will and loving our neighbors by helping them alleviate their suffering, even if it causes us to take on suffering ourselves, then we will not be saved regardless of the religion we profess. St. Paul pointed this out to the Romans, writing, "All who sin outside the law will also perish without reference to it, and all who sin under the law will be judged in accordance with it. For it is not those who hear the law who are just in the sight of God; rather, those who observe the law will be justified" (Rom. 2:12-13).

The Church was commissioned by the risen Christ to carry out three distinct roles (Matt. 28:18-20). She teaches us about the nature and motivations of God as taught by Christ Himself; she evangelizes by witnessing to these truths to all who will listen; and she administers the sacraments that provide the graces required for humans to become like God, because we cannot do that without His help. God utilizes secondary sources to carry out His plans in general, and by using fellow humans to make known His desires for us, speaking in terms of earthly life, He makes His providential plans more easily relatable to us (CCC 306).

Indeed, Pope Paul VI wrote that "the sharing in the divine nature given to men through the grace of Christ bears a certain likeness to the origin, development, and nourishing of natural life. The faithful are born anew by Baptism, strengthened by the sacrament of Confirmation, and receive in the Eucharist the food of eternal life. By means of these sacraments of Christian initiation, they thus receive in increasing measure the treasures of the divine life and advance toward the perfection of charity" (CCC 1212). It is this sacramental economy that ultimately provides the most significant advantage to those who enter the Catholic Church in all her fullness.

The Church's sacramental system works in both directions. God, through the Church, makes His graces available to us, but to receive them, we must request them and enter into them worthily. If we are baptized, we enter the state of grace, which means we have accepted God's invitation and want to live with Him forever according to His direction. To be baptized in the Church is tantamount to a personal repudiation of Original Sin and would be equivalent to the Prodigal Son returning to his father.

We need to reconcile with God if we fall from grace through mortal sin, which is to say we do something purposely opposing God's will in an important matter with full knowledge of what we are doing. No one acts that way toward someone they truly love. No loving spouse would ever deliberately oppose their spouse's wishes in a serious matter or put someone else's well-being ahead of that of their spouse. Having betrayed your spouse's trust even once, you would find it to be very difficult to regain your previous relationship.

Not so with God. In His infinite mercy, God has made it rather simple to return to the state of grace for Catholics, consistent with His goal of uniting with us after death. We need only to partake of the sacrament of Reconciliation, which involves an act of contrition, a confessing of our sins to a priest, and his absolution pending a penance (CCC 1468–1469). To stay in the state of grace, we must avoid further mortal sin, thereby demonstrating our love and fidelity to God and His Church.

Non-Christians who know of Christ must join His Body, the Church, through Baptism prior to death to publicly proclaim that they want to spend an eternity with Him. After all, if they shun His Church, which is His Body, they also shun Christ. However, there are sometimes extenuating circumstances, and God is just and all-knowing, so the Church assumes that our Creator will make the necessary accommodations for people as He sees fit—God is not bound by His sacraments (CCC 1257).

For instance, "the Church has always held the firm conviction that those who suffer death for the sake of the faith without having received Baptism are baptized by their death for and with Christ. This Baptism of blood, like the desire for Baptism, brings about the fruits of Baptism without being a sacrament" (CCC 1258). Likewise, "for catechumens who die before their Baptism, their explicit desire to receive it, together with repentance for their sins, and charity, assures them the salvation that they were not able to receive through the sacrament" (CCC 1259). Finally, the Church holds:

> "since Christ died for all, and since all men are in fact called to one and the same destiny, which is divine, we [the Church] must hold that the Holy Spirit offers to all the possibility of being made partakers, in a way known to God, of the Paschal mystery." Every man who is ignorant of the Gospel of Christ and of his Church, but seeks the truth and does the will of God in accordance with his understanding of it, can be saved. It may be supposed that such persons would have desired Baptism explicitly if they had known its necessity. (CCC 1260)

This is important to those who are dying because it establishes a basis for understanding that God is indeed all-powerful and loves us more than we love ourselves. It militates against the view that, because there is evil in the world, God, the Creator of the universe, is not powerful enough to stop it or has ceased to love us.

It opens the door to understanding evil, suffering, and death in a different, more positive way as tools used by God to lead us back to Him. It also shows God's infinite mercy and His willingness to forgive any sin if we make the effort to repent.

Chapter 3

Understanding Our Role in God's Plan

One of the key concerns of most people facing death is their standing with God, both generically as a human and specifically as an individual. When we suffer, we are often worried that God has abandoned us or is punishing us for some sin, which we may or may not acknowledge. The scriptural book of Job deals with this problem directly, and there are many other references in the Church's teaching on the role of humanity in God's plan that show this concern is simply not true.

God Loves Humanity

We will start with the fact that God created everything for man (CCC 358), who is the summit of the Creator's work (CCC 343), as shown in the Creation account, which notes that man is made in the image of God and is the only creature rated by God to be *very* good (Gen. 1:26-31). Of all the visible creatures, man alone has the ability to reason and was given free will so that he can know and freely love God (CCC 356). Man is also the only creature with a material body and a spiritual soul, which unites the spiritual and material worlds within his nature (CCC 355). Where every other visible creature has only its temporal existence in a mortal body, man is the composite of a mortal body and a spiritual soul, and thus has the potential to live forever as spirit. Man is the only creature that God willed for his own sake (CCC 356). All other material creatures are destined for the good of the human race (CCC 353). Therefore, death to a man does not have the same ramifications as does the death of an animal, whose body will be used for food, fur, or fertilizer to benefit man directly or indirectly.

God left the universe in an unfinished, imperfect state and gave man dominion over it to perfect it for his use and that of his neighbors (CCC 307). The point was not to perfect the universe but to perfect man, so that he can learn to share in the divine nature—loving God, his neighbors, and himself fully and unconditionally. In giving him dominion over creation, God gave man a purpose and an opportunity to show love to the rest of creation.

God also gave him Eve to teach them both what it meant to love one another (Gen. 2:21–24). They were each given deficiencies that the other fills to teach them that they are not self-reliant but need to cooperate in order to be successful. This is made most obvious in the marital act, which requires the mutual self-giving of the spouses to procreate (CCC 2366).

When I say that God made everything good for its purpose, I mean that His plan extends to every human. No matter how disabled a person appears, each of us was made perfectly for the role we've been assigned in God's plan. This does not mean that people do not have skill or resource gaps; it just means that they will have what they need to fulfill their roles.

Sometimes, like in parenting, this requires the cooperation of two or more people, but that too is part of God's plan. Every person can give and receive love, and every person has a unique place in God's plan. In this way, God values diversity over equality—no two things He has made are ever exactly the same. Nevertheless, we all have equal dignity as children of God, from the person with the greatest skills and responsibilities to the one who is completely dependent on others, and we will be judged based on whether we have demonstrated love in fulfilling our particular role in providence, God's plan for the salvation of men.

As discussed above, the Church teaches that God's main desire is for man to become like Him and to join Him in eternal bliss in Heaven. He apparently hard-coded that desire into the human will, because man has desired to be like God since the beginning. It was this desire that Satan used to entice Eve to take the forbidden fruit (Gen. 3:1–6). Indeed, there are stories about men aspiring to be gods in most, if not every, culture. In ancient Rome, the emperors would declare themselves gods. And in modern pop culture, there is a pantheon of movies based on superheroes with godlike powers. St. Thomas Aquinas explains that this phenomenon means everything desires its own perfection, and, in man, this desire is to be like God.[12]

The Fall of Man

It might be surprising to some that Adam and Eve were thrown out of Eden for trying to become like God, since God wanted that for them too. It seems clear they were not ready to love as God loves and were too self-centered and too impatient to recognize that God was training them to become like Him. As the Church puts it, "he [man] wanted to 'be like God' but 'without God, before God, and not in accordance with God'" (CCC 398). Our first parents were, in fact, unfaithful to God, preferring Satan's half-truths to God's truthful counsel (Gen. 3:1–6).

---

[12] *ST* I, q. 6, art. 1, resp. to obj. 2.

Up to that point, Adam and Eve had been coddled, having no needs that God did not provide for. They had not yet felt the sting of suffering to redirect them from evil, since God gave them original justice, harmony with the rest of creation, to keep them out of harm's way (CCC 400). Now, separated from God by choice, and no longer showered with His benevolence, men first had unfulfilled needs and felt suffering to warn them about those needs.

This all came about as a consequence of man's separation from God, not because God was showing any malice toward His creatures. The Church teaches that Adam and Eve immediately lost their original holiness, which caused them to fear God, since Satan had convinced them that God was jealous of His prerogatives (CCC 399). They lost the harmony of original justice by being disobedient to God, and without it, the body is no longer governed by the spiritual faculties and becomes disordered, degenerating until it dies. Without harmony with nature, man's control over the land becomes strained, and decay begins to creep in (CCC 400).

God's Recovery Plan

At just the right time in human history, "God became man so that we might become God," as St. Athanasius stated so eloquently in the fourth century after Jesus Christ was born (CCC 460). God sent His Son in human form to demonstrate what we should be and what we should do to share in the divine nature. Jesus gave us the Beatitudes to teach us what that nature entailed. We killed Him for His kindness, and yet He rose from the dead to demonstrate His divinity, validate His teaching, and show us the depth of God's love for us—and mercy beyond even that of the father in the parable of the Prodigal Son. As Jesus Himself taught, "No one has greater love than this, to lay down one's life for one's friends"

(John 15:13). Can there be any doubt that Jesus loves us as does His and our Father?

God made us in His image, and He respects our rights as sentient beings to be self-directing, giving us the choice of joining Him forever in His Kingdom, where everyone admitted will love perfectly, where there is no sin, suffering, or death to separate ourselves from Him. Every action is toward that goal of bringing us into the Kingdom despite all our transgressions (CCC 313). Indeed, He has put the entire universe in place to help us make that decision and to give us the opportunity to learn to act prudently, aligned with His will. This is clearly the plan of a loving and merciful God, who has our best interests at heart. These words do not describe a God who would maliciously make us suffer or who does not care about us. Clearly, He does care for us—deeply. As we shall soon see, His loving plan for us includes the use of suffering to provide clear direction for activities that teach us to love fully and unconditionally—and to give us a view of what life would be without His guidance and the four last things (death, judgment, Heaven, and Hell) to provide motivation for sharing in the divine nature and giving meaning to how we live our lives. This reemphasizes that God makes everything perfect for its purpose, which is ultimately for the perfection and the deification of man, even those things that cause us discomfort on earth.

Suffering and Death

The fact that suffering and death are actually instruments of God's mercy and forgiveness is obscured from the secular man, who only believes what his senses can detect. This is because our suffering, while deliberately unpleasant to motivate us to seek the good we lack, directs us toward a redemption that is not of this world but rather in the world to come, which we cannot sense directly without special gifts. If we rely solely on the senses, we only perceive the discomfort of suffering. But if we take the time to contemplate why we suffer with the perspective that God is good and all-powerful, we can perceive the ways God uses suffering to perfect us and to lead us to Himself. Granted, not everyone is capable of this kind of analysis. Instead, we can, of course, choose to believe the witness of Christ and the Church He commissioned to spread the good news about God's mercy and forgiveness and His desire for humanity to return to Him. God is good and, in His mercy, allows each of us to choose our own path. He invites all to join His Church and, by extension, His Kingdom. We have only to say yes.

In the book of Job, we learn that Job was the most righteous man on earth, used by God as an example of fidelity to others. When God allows Satan to kill all his children and destroy all his wealth, Job responds, "Naked I came forth from my mother's womb, and naked shall I go back there. The Lord gave and the Lord has taken away; blessed be the name of the Lord!" (Job 1:21). God points this out to Satan, who responds by saying that if Job was deprived of health, he would turn on God. God gives Satan permission to torture Job but not to kill him. Satan responds by inflicting Job with severe boils from the soles of his feet to the crown of his head. Seeing his agony, Job's wife tells him to let go of his innocence, curse God, and die. Job answers her, "We accept good things from God; should we not accept evil?" (Job 2:10).

Job is then visited by three friends, who sit silently with him for seven days and nights to support him in his suffering. They find their voices after hearing Job curse his birth, recommending that Job confess his sins and seek mercy from God. Job, however, is sure of his innocence and demands a hearing from God because he too assumes that his suffering is punishment for some sin. Through three cycles of speeches, Job's friends press him to end his suffering by admitting his guilt and asking God for forgiveness. Job is steadfast in proclaiming his innocence, to the point that his friends reprove him for assuming he is more righteous than God (Job 2–37).

God then addresses Job directly, reminding Job that God is responsible for all the workings of the universe and asking Job whether he could do the same. Job, humbled by the experience, responds, "I know that you can do all things, and that no purpose of yours can be hindered.... I have spoken but did not understand; things too marvelous for me, which I did not know.... By hearsay I had heard of you, but now my eye has seen you. Therefore I disown what I have said, and repent in dust and ashes" (Job 38–42:6).

In the epilogue of the story, the Lord restores Job's reputation as a righteous man, telling his three friends that they must ask Job to pray for them because they have "not spoken rightly concerning me, as has my servant Job" (Job 42:8). They had assumed that his suffering was punishment for some evil, which Job had steadfastly denied. Everything Job lost God replaces twofold, and He gives him twice the normal expected longevity.

The key takeaway from this is that suffering is not necessarily a punishment (although it can be), and its presence should not be presumed as guilt on the part of the sufferer. Indeed, Job suffered precisely because he was the most righteous person on earth. God chose him to suffer for the benefit of others so they could have a better understanding of the nature of God, as well as an example of how to suffer faithfully. Job's suffering is redemptive; in his case, he was rewarded temporally so the people could see it, and, presumably, also in the afterlife, which the original audience for the story did not yet understand.

Do not worry that God has forgotten you in your time of need. He has not. He made the whole universe for us, and He longs for each of us to return to Him. Rest assured that suffering is not a measure of His displeasure with us. As in the case of Job, He could be very pleased with us and sees fit to use us to save others. Like Job, we should be prepared to accept the evil and the good we receive in life and trust that God always has our best interests in mind in either case. This is especially true when we are subject to suffering. It takes great faith and hope to persist in love when we are suffering, but sometimes that's what it takes to bring others to God. If we suffer willingly for the benefit of others according to God's will, then we will be glorified with Christ on the Last Day.

One final critical point is that humans cannot aspire to become gods on our own. The vocation to eternal life is supernatural. It depends entirely on grace, because God alone can reveal and give Himself. Indeed, it surpasses the power of human intellect and will (CCC 1998). "Grace is *favor*, the *free and undeserved help* that God gives us to respond to His call to become children of God, adoptive sons, partakers of the divine nature and eternal life" (CCC 1996).

> God's free initiative demands *man's free response*, for God has created man in his image by conferring on him, along with freedom, the power to know him and love him. The soul only enters freely into the communion of love. God immediately touches and directly moves the heart of man. He has placed in man a longing for truth and goodness that only He can satisfy. (CCC 2002)

Said differently, God takes the initiative in every relationship. He calls to us, and we have the choice of saying yes or no. Then He provides the help with grace to fulfill what we set out to do. God makes it possible to do the impossible because His love for us is so great.

Chapter 4

God Uses Evil and Suffering to Bring about Greater Good

The basic plot of many works of art, including books, plays, and movies, is good versus evil. Although good inevitably wins because that is what the public demands, these stories misrepresent the nature of evil and can make it difficult to see things as they really are. This new solution to why bad things happen to good people requires a reevaluation of how we view evil and suffering. St. John Paul II provides the critical insight in his 1984 apostolic letter *Salvifici Doloris*, which explores the Christian meaning of human suffering. Contrary to common assumptions, what we consider to be evil does not necessarily oppose good. Sure, evil is defined as something undesirable, and goods are desirable, seemingly in opposition. However, lacking the foresight of God, what we see as harmful might be medicinal.

In fact, evil only exists as the absence of good, in form (what it is), function (what it does), or order (where it fits in God's plan), to use the philosophical characterization for all things. Of these, only disordered choices are sinful and opposed to goodness, because they involve choosing a lesser good over a greater one. On the other hand, it is considered an evil if something is corrupted (like wine turning into vinegar) or fails to function properly. These are privations of good but are not sinful when they occur naturally. As St. John Paul II explains, "Christianity proclaims the essential good of existence and the good of that which exists, acknowledges the goodness of the Creator and proclaims the goodness of creatures."[13] St. Thomas, echoing St. Augustine, agrees, describing evil in his *Summa Theologiae* as "the privation of good, like darkness is the absence of light."[14]

St. John Paul II reset the statement of the problem of evil, pointing out that "man suffers because of a good in which he does not share, from which in a certain sense he is cut off, or of which he has deprived himself. He particularly suffers when he ought—in the normal order of things—to share in this good and does not have it."[15] Looked at from this perspective, it is easy to find numerous reasons that a loving God would have to withhold goods from someone. Certainly, it is a lot easier to understand why a loving God might withhold good from a person for his or her benefit than to understand how a loving God would inflict evil on someone, even if they mean the same thing technically. This is because the term *inflict evil* implies malicious intent, whereas *withholding good* does not. There is no malice in God, only love, so it is appropriate to consider in this way.

Loving parents withhold goods from their children for a variety of good reasons. Sometimes the good parent might think that making children work for what they want is good training and will make a child appreciate and value the desired good more. Sometimes the

---

[13] John Paul II, apostolic letter *Salvifici Doloris* (On the Christian Meaning of Human Suffering) (February 11, 1984), no. 7.
[14] *ST* I, q., 48, art. 1.
[15] John Paul II, *Salvifici Doloris*, no. 7

child is just not ready to handle the responsibilities associated with the desired good. Other times, the parent might conclude that the desired good is really not good for the child and withholds it. For example, many parents withhold cell phones from their preteen children to prevent them from being exposed to harmful things or be distracted from the goods they should be pursuing. Finally, loving parents will discipline their child to teach the child how to interact properly with others. This punishment might entail withholding a physical good, like dessert or access to the Internet or television, or it might be withholding some of their freedom, like with a "time-out," grounding, or curfew. In each of these examples, the parent withheld a good from a child, out of love and not out of malice. The same type of logic is appropriately applied to our heavenly Father because He will withhold goods, an action we might see as evil, until the exact time and situation that they are most useful.

In *When Bad Things Happen to Good People*, Rabbi Kushner speaks for people that see this as mere wordsmanship, saying:

> Sometimes in our cleverness we try to persuade ourselves that what we call evil is not real, does not exist, but is only a condition of not enough goodness, even as "cold" means "not enough heat" or darkness is a name we give to the absence of light. We may thus prove that there is really no such thing as darkness or cold, but people do stumble and hurt themselves because of the dark and people do die of exposure to cold. Their deaths and injuries are no less real because of our verbal cleverness.[16]

We do not minimize the injuries and deaths caused by evil. What we do is note that if it is the responsibility of God, some

---

[16] Kushner, *Bad Things*, 27–28.

opportunity for spiritual growth will be somehow entwined in the problem's solution that is more valuable than the related temporal suffering. Rabbi Kushner tells his readers that "belief in a world to come where the innocent are compensated for their suffering can help people endure the unfairness of life without losing faith. But it can also be an excuse for not being troubled or outraged by injustice around us and not using our God-given intelligence to try to do something about it."[17]

In counter to this argument, know that we can believe God will compensate in Heaven those of us who suffer unjustly, while we heed our suffering on earth, taking action to remove or at least avoid the evils that suffering has detected. There is no reason that both cannot be true simultaneously. In fact, that is what is recommended. We can and should address the sources of suffering on earth—otherwise the suffering is pointless, as Rabbi Kushner points out. But there are many cases where humans cannot correct injustices or where God uses us to save others. In these situations, we rely on God's mercy to bring the innocent to Himself, where joy will overwhelm any negative residual effects of earthly suffering.

All evils can be expressed as the absence of some good. For instance, a thunderstorm forms when there is moisture, an energy source, and an absence of atmospheric stability.[18] This instability is caused when hot and cold fronts collide, events that are part of complex cyclical patterns that have evolved since the atmosphere was formed. God, with perfect foresight, could set up these cycles so they could intersect and cause storms at the times they were

---

[17] Ibid., 29.
[18] "Understanding Lightning: Thunderstorm Development," National Weather Service, https://www.weather.gov/safety/lightning -thunderstorm-development.

needed. If He decides later to calm a storm, like Jesus did on the lake of Galilee, He needs to stabilize the atmosphere, which He can do with only a command: "Be still" (Mark4:39). This is just another manifestation of God's creative power. Since evil is the absence of good, God can bring goodness from it by supplying what is lacking. God, who can make anything out of nothing with just His word, is not deterred from doing so but chooses the best time in which to make things happen according to His plan. Remember, God is in complete control of the arc of history, with nothing escaping His notice or being too hard for Him to accomplish. The Church, in fact, recognizes that:

> With infinite wisdom and goodness God freely willed to create a world "in a state of journeying" toward its ultimate perfection. In God's plan this process of becoming involves the appearance of certain beings and the disappearance of others, the existence of the more perfect alongside the less perfect, both constructive and destructive forces of nature. With physical good there exists also physical evil as long as creation has not reached perfection. (CCC 310)

Note that there is a nomenclature difference in my work versus the *Catechism*. Because they have different sources, I separate evils caused by the environment as physical evils and those associated with living creatures as natural evils, while the *Catechism* combines them all as physical evil. This passage from the *Catechism* includes a recognition of the evolution of living species, including the appearance of certain beings and the disappearance of others, which I have categorized as natural evils.

It is quite clear from the above that God willed both physical and natural evils, not out of malice to man but because He makes effective use of both to bring about the salvation of men. God can use physical evil to redirect us from gathering impermanent material wealth to pursuing eternal wealth — for example, using a storm to destroy the property we had expected to sustain us, forcing us to see the unreliability of trusting in material wealth that is here today and gone tomorrow. At the same time, He uses physical evils to challenge us to grow and use our skills and resources to mold the universe as His stewards of creation, giving us purpose and training us to be the best versions of ourselves. Natural evils, mostly diseases, kill 90 percent of the population and so are vivid reminders to us that we are mortal.[19] They also give us a chance to help one another to reach salvation as we care for each other and help one other recuperate from injury or illness.

In reality, the only type of evil with malicious intent is the evil of sin. Sin is a disordered choice, picking the lesser good over a greater one. In the human experience, this is typically making choices that benefit ourselves at the expense of the good of others, in direct contrast to the love that God wants from us. Sin began originally when Eve chose to believe Satan over God on the ramifications of eating the forbidden fruit from the tree of the knowledge of good and evil, followed closely by Adam's choice to please his wife rather than please God (Gen. 3:1-6). By these actions, humans separated themselves from God, who anticipated our sins and had planned for our redemption from the beginning. When He warned our first parents that they would suffer and die if they ate the fruit, He was telling them the extent of the recovery plan that

---

[19] "Global Health Estimates 2019: Estimated Deaths by Cause and Region, 2000 and 2019," World Health Organization, https://cdn.who.int/media/docs/default-source/gho-documents/global-health-estimates/ghe2019_cod_wbincome_2000_201933383745-a750-4d94-8491-fb209dcece6f_7c1ac8d4-d425-4deb-8a12-1dc26c293e80.xlsx?sfvrsn=e7bafa8_9.

would be necessary to reconcile, not threatening to destroy them. Remember, there is no malice in God, only love.

Many will find it shocking or even scandalous that a loving God would use evil as a tool to bring about His goals for humanity. But the truth is that God's perspective is greater than ours, and thus what we perceive as evil might actually be good for us. St. Thomas Aquinas gives us the mental tools to evaluate why and how that could be. He notes that no rational being would choose evil on its own merits but that they would choose it if it were attached to a good greater than the good to which it was a privation.[20] For instance, God would choose the evil of punishment because He values justice, the good attached to punishment,

[20] *ST* I, q. 19, art. 9: "Since the ratio of good is the ratio of appetibility, as said before (I:5:1), and since evil is opposed to good, it is impossible that any evil, as such, should be sought for by the appetite, either natural, or animal, or by the intellectual appetite which is the will. Nevertheless, evil may be sought accidentally, so far as it accompanies a good, as appears in each of the appetites. For a natural agent intends not privation or corruption, but the form to which is annexed the privation of some other form, and the generation of one thing, which implies the corruption of another. Also, when a lion kills a stag, his object is food, to obtain which the killing of the animal is only the means. Similarly, the fornicator has merely pleasure for his object, and the deformity of sin is only an accompaniment. Now the evil that accompanies one good, is the privation of another good. Never therefore would evil be sought after, not even accidentally, unless the good that accompanies the evil were more desired than the good of which the evil is the privation. Now God wills no good more than He wills His own goodness; yet He wills one good more than another. Hence, He in no way wills the evil of sin, which is the privation of right order towards the divine good. The evil of natural defect, or of punishment, He does will, by willing the good to which such evils are attached. Thus, in willing justice He wills punishment;

more than He values the comfort of the sinner, the good that is lost with punishment.[21] In a similar way, He chooses to have physical evils because He values His universal plan of evolving the universe to perfection, and the opportunities it provides to redirect and train humanity to love and care for our environment and each other, greater than He values human temporal comfort, the good that is lost to physical evil, which God knows is transitory. Natural evils, which ultimately culminate in death, exist because we need to die to make room for subsequent generations until the full population of the new heaven and the new earth are filled on the Last Day.

St. Thomas also recognizes that God does not wish anyone to sin, because it results in the separation of one of His children from Him, which is counter to His greatest wish—to be reunited with us in eternity.[22] The good attached to sin is free will, and while highly valued as a precursor to true love, which must be freely given, it is not valued higher than the loss of love itself, which is the result of sin.

Despite not wishing anyone to sin, God does allow us to sin, sometimes horrendously, because free will is necessarily attached to the possibility of errant choices. However, our Creator actively works to help man avoid sinful choices by making sinful choices uncomfortable through suffering. God is merciful, forgiving all that repent sacramentally, but He also warns through Scripture that unrepentant sinners will have no place in His Kingdom (1 Cor. 6:9-10; Gal. 5:19-21; Eph. 5:3-5).

---

and in willing the preservation of the natural order, He wills some things to be naturally corrupted."

[21] Ibid.

[22] Ibid.

The Church herself acknowledges that God uses evil to bring about good, stating in the *Catechism*:

> In time we can discover that God in his almighty providence can bring a good from the consequences of an evil, even a moral evil, caused by his creatures: "It was not you," said Joseph to his brothers, "who sent me here, but God. You meant evil against me; but God meant it for good, to bring it about that many people should be kept alive." From the greatest moral evil ever committed—the rejection and murder of God's only Son, caused by the sins of all men—God, by his grace that "abounded all the more," brought the greatest of goods: the glorification of Christ and our redemption. But for all that, evil never becomes a good. (CCC 312)

Perhaps the best example of how God uses evil in His plans is the story of the reluctant prophet, Jonah, who has been commissioned to preach repentance to the Ninevites. Jonah does not want to help his enemies, so he boards a ship going in the opposite direction. God calls up a storm to change the environment (using physical evil). This storm causes the sailors to question who is at fault. Jonah admits his responsibility and tells the sailors to throw him overboard (sin). God causes the storm to stop, which causes the sailors to convert (healing). God then causes the whale to swallow Jonah (natural evil) and then to spit him on shore. Jonah is asked again to preach repentance to the Ninevites; this time he agrees. Much to his dismay, the Ninevites listen to Jonah and repent at his story (Jon. 1–4).

There are a couple of important concepts contained in this biblical story. The first is that we would think of this as God reacting to Jonah's actions as they happen because that is how we would have to do it. Actually, God could foresee this happening before He created the world, so He could have anticipated the events and had the storm come up as part of His original plan when He set up the weather patterns. Notice, too, that God deftly changes the environment to prompt each of the people in this story to make the move that is natural to them. There is no coercion; everyone acts freely. Faced with the storm, the sailors naturally change course and ask themselves what prompted the fury of the storm. Jonah, being a good man, recognizes that his actions put the others at risk and seeks to save them by being thrown overboard. God, anticipating this, shifted the weather patterns to calm the storm and bring the whale to the area to save His reluctant prophet.

Interestingly, God's plan anticipated Jonah's initial resistance and utilized it to make him more effective. It gave Jonah a mighty tale to tell the Ninevites in support of his preaching. In addition, the plan now had a whole ship full of corroborating witnesses who were in town and certainly telling anyone who would listen about their adventure. No wonder the Ninevites converted. Indeed, God's plans are efficient and often serve multiple purposes. As it turns out, when the scribes and Pharisees press Jesus for a sign, He is able to reference this well-known story to deflect their request and use it as a basis for teaching them and all future readers, saying:

An evil and unfaithful generation seeks a sign, but no sign will be given it except the sign of Jonah the prophet. Just as Jonah was in the belly of the whale three days and three nights, so will the Son of Man be in the heart of the earth three days and three nights. At the judgment, the men of Nineveh will arise with this generation and condemn it, because they repented at the preaching of Jonah; and there is something greater than Jonah here. (Matt. 12:39–41)

Chapter 5

Suffering and Its Four Tasks

Having demonstrated both God's greatness and His love for mankind, we must rethink suffering. To be consistent with our developed view of God, suffering (and death) must bring about man's return to God. Now, the biggest impediment most people have in understanding suffering and death is that they believe that they are evil, and that evil is opposed to good. But as I have explained, evil is not opposed to good—evil is the privation (lack or loss) of an expected good, just as darkness is the absence of light and silence is the absence of sound.[23]

The second problem is that most people conflate suffering and evil, which is incorrect. Suffering is our ability to detect evil. As described in more depth in *Why All People Suffer*,[24] suffering is a gift from God that warns us when we are threatened by evil, which, reflecting the above, should be understood to mean that suffering identifies when we are threatened by the lack of a critical good. For instance, hunger is not what threatens us; it is the warning

---

[23] John Paul II, *Salvifici Doloris*, no. 7.
[24] Paul Chaloux, *Why All People Suffer: How a Loving God Uses Suffering to Perfect Us* (Manchester, NH: Sophia Institute Press, 2021).

signal we get when we need to eat. What threatens us is the lack of food to fuel our bodies. Similarly, pain alerts us to the loss of bodily integrity caused by some injury.

St. John Paul II introduced this concept in his apostolic letter *Salvifici Doloris*, pointing out that suffering is experiencing a feeling with any kind of evil. The pope notes that, in the Old Testament language, the vocabulary did not distinguish between suffering and evil, but that Greek has a verb that means "I experience a feeling, I suffer." Because of this, as he points out, "suffering is no longer directly identifiable with (objective) evil but expresses a situation in which man experiences evil and in doing so becomes the subject of suffering."[25]

Said another way, suffering is the generic term for the sensation we get when we lack a critical need. In practice, these suffering sensations are specific enough that we can often identify what we are missing. For instance, if we lose a loved one, we feel lonely. If we miss a meal, we feel hungry. If our body's integrity is lost through injury, we will feel pain. If our digestive system is not working properly, we will feel nauseous. If we lack God in our lives, we may have a sort of empty feeling, like something is missing. In each case, suffering is highlighting a loss or lack of some basic need and alerting us to it, and everyone can tell the difference between feeling hungry, lonely, nauseous, or in pain, or that feeling of spiritual emptiness. These feelings are all deliberately unpleasant to us to motivate us to avoid the evil and obtain the missing good that we require.

In truth, suffering does far more for us than just detecting and identifying the evil that threatens us. Suffering has a prominent role in providence, God's great plan for the universe, and it is

[25] John Paul II, *Salvifici Doloris*, no. 7.

undeniably linked to death. In fact, suffering warns us that we are dying and gives us time and the motivation to prepare ourselves and our loved ones for our deaths. Because it is unpleasant, suffering is effective at motivating us to attain the required good to resolve the suffering. In this way, suffering is directive, making bad choices unappealing because they cause suffering and good choices appealing because they resolve the suffering by attaining the missing good. There are four tasks of suffering to bring a person from sin to salvation, from unbelief to sharing in the divine nature, if we heed their messages. Each of these tasks comes into play in terminal suffering. Recognizing them for what they are and responding appropriately can make a huge difference in the outlook of both patients and caregivers.

The first task is to take us from vice to virtue, teaching us proper self-love. This task is completed with simple cause-and-effect feedback loops that everyone on earth experiences. If we are hungry, the hunger motivates us to eat. If we are in pain, we will try to heal the wound. When a person is doing something that is harmful to himself, suffering provides a cause-and-effect feedback loop that dissuades the person from doing further self-harm. For instance, if a person drinks too much, he will get sick and have a hangover the next morning. If the person does not drink the next night, he will wake up sober and, perhaps, chastened to the point where he will be more diligent about monitoring his drinking and become temperate.

People learn justice in much the same way. If they treat someone unfairly, the other person will suffer and object, transferring at least a portion of the suffering back to the unjust. Their objections, which can be anything from lawsuits and forceable seizure of the good in question to a simple hurt look from the person treated unfairly, cause some discomfort, which most people will try to avoid in future dealings. When you continue to carry on with your life despite suffering, you learn fortitude. The cause-and-effect loops that make up the first task are repeated daily around the world by people of all faiths and those of no faith until they are prudent and make decisions that no longer cause them to suffer. This has been going on for thousands of years because the great Greek and Roman philosophers recognized and highly valued these same cardinal virtues: fortitude, temperance, justice, and prudence.

And the suffering related to these cause-and-effect loops does not stop just because you are terminally ill. In fact, it escalates in intensity because the threats to your existence are growing stronger. If you are missing any of the five basic needs all people have—I go over them in detail in chapter 16—you will experience a corresponding feeling to let you know what is lacking.[26] Suffering will guide both the patient and the caregiver to take care of themselves, making it uncomfortable when they do not. For instance, if the patient is lonely, she needs more social stimulation. This must be communicated to the caregiver to rectify, and the caregiver, acting in love, should help the patient engage with others. On the other hand, if the caregiver is feeling burned out, she should heed the suffering and get help.

The second task of suffering is to reorient us toward God. It is a call to conversion. This generally works in one of two ways. The easy, incremental way is via the first task, which as we have just discussed, builds virtue by way of simple cause-and-effect feedback

[26] The five things all people are concerned with are their physical pain, uncertainty about their medical prognosis, concern about their purpose in life, concern about their social status, and concern about what will happen after they die (their spiritual status).

loops. For example, if you mistreat people and they rebel against you, you learn justice. Eventually a person learns what to do to avoid or alleviate suffering; this good judgment is called prudence. A prudent person will come to understand that prudence is aligning oneself to God and will seek out other people who have come to similar conclusions and join a church. This step may be motivated by a feeling of spiritual emptiness that requires engaging with God and His Church to resolve. This task applies equally to the caregiver and the patient, and each can help the other reach out to God. While caregivers will have access to more catechetical information, patients will have more time and motivation to contemplate the existential questions and can, in fact, initiate the discussion of God and the mysteries of suffering and death with their caregivers. If a patient is a devout follower of God and His Church and can show joy in the midst of pain, it will leave an indelible impression on the onlookers, including the caregiver, potentially leading to conversions of heart.

The second way suffering leads one to God is through overwhelming force, where it becomes obvious that God exists and is the only one who can resolve an issue. St. Paul required such a conversion experience, having to be knocked off his horse and blinded on the road to Damascus, before he could see the light (Acts 9:1–19). Others may have to endure the loss of certain possessions or people that are distracting them from becoming the best version of themselves. Without these distractions, the person will naturally contemplate what is important to fill that gap and may find the answer in God. A similar dynamic occurs with significant illnesses or injuries that force a person to slow down and take stock of his or her life. The Church's experience is that "very often illness provokes a search for God and a return to him" (CCC 1501). The reason the search for God will be successful is that God is continually reaching out to us all, just as the father of the Prodigal Son did in Jesus' parable (Luke 15:20).

The third task of suffering is to unleash our love of neighbor when we see them suffer. Suffering brings out the empathy and compassion a person has within him and allows people to both love and be loved. St. John Paul II, in talking about this task, points out that Jesus has two parables that show how this works and what the reward is.[27] These are the parable of the Good Samaritan (Luke 10:29-37) and the parable of the Last Judgment (Matt. 25:31-46). In the first story, the focus is on a man who has been beaten, robbed, and left for dead on the side of the road. Two Jewish leaders pass him by and do not stop to help. But a nameless Samaritan stops out of true altruism and cares for the man, who is a Jew and, therefore, technically an enemy warrior. St. John Paul II emphasizes that we need to love our friends and neighbors, caring for them, as the Good Samaritan did. He then pivots to the parable of the Last Judgment, where Jesus says that, on the Last Day, He will separate everyone, sending to His Father those who showed mercy to the suffering and sending to Hell those who did not exhibit such mercy to their fellow men. St. John Paul II then makes the point that unless our love is unleashed like it was in the Good Samaritan, we cannot enter the Kingdom of Heaven.[28]

Now, it may seem that the caregiver has the opportunity to unleash his love on the patient but that the patient does not have the opportunity to reciprocate. This, however, could not be further from the truth. We are all called to love, and illness and injury provide abundant opportunities to show that love. The caregiver is confronted with the same opportunity as the Good Samaritan.

[27] John Paul II, *Salvifici Doloris*, no. 30.
[28] Ibid.

He sees someone suffering and answers God's call to care for his neighbor. The patient is analogous to the injured man lying naked by the edge of the road in the parable. Would it really be too much to ask of the patient to be kind and pleasant toward the caregiver and also to pray for his good? As the patient, you can react with love for your caregiver, doing whatever you can to lighten his load, or you can treat him like he owes it to you to care for you. The truth is, even if he does owe it to you, you should act in love for the sake of God, to whom we owe everything we have and are.

The fourth task of suffering is to teach us redemptive love, to love as Jesus did, willing to suffer for the benefit of others. This is the highest form of love because it is self-sacrificial, putting others before yourself, and it requires the person's love and faith in the goodness and reliability of God to be strong enough to suffer and potentially die for the benefit of another. This is the point at which people cross over from good to holy, worried no longer for themselves but for the good of others, trusting in the promises of Christ. This is the best version of oneself, able to love completely and unconditionally, sharing in the divine nature as described by Christ in the Beatitudes (Matt. 5:1-9; CCC 1718-1723). This fourth task allows one to conquer death in emulation of Jesus, who first accomplished this (1 Cor. 15:26). Death no longer has a hold on you if you cease to fear it.

The existence of redemptive suffering is extremely important in God's plan. It is the ultimate display of love, which is to wish the good of another, even at the cost of our own suffering and, potentially, death. It is how Jesus, true God and true man, reconciled humanity with God, opening Heaven while providing us with a model of the holiness required to be in the presence of God for eternity (CCC 457-459). In doing so, He demonstrated the depth of God's love for humanity and His desire for man to share in His divinity (CCC 458–460). Echoing the insight of St. Irenaeus in the first century, the Church teaches that "God became man so that we might become God" (CCC 460).

The fact that suffering, if borne on the behalf of others, is redemptive is another sign of the consistent, loving nature of God. He rewards what He values, and He values love above all. He shows us this in family life. First, He chose to bring forth new life through the mutual self-giving of a husband and wife, who then sacrifice further to raise their children and, in some cases, to care for their elderly parents. True love always requires sacrifice on the part of the lovers for the good of the ones they love. If they are not willing to engage in sacrificial love, then they are not yet prepared to enter the Kingdom of God.

It should be noted at this point that charity (theological love) is a theological virtue, a gift from God that is infused within us, as are the other two theological virtues of hope and faith (CCC 1813). In this, it differs from human virtues that we gain through effort and repetition. Suffering does not drive the development of the love of God like it does the human virtues that lead to proper self-love. It instead provides the opportunity for true love to manifest itself in the aid of the suffering. In the third task, our suffering triggers compassion and empathy in those properly disposed to it, and they will come to our aid.

When the love within us is strong enough, we will start to recognize opportunities for spiritual growth through redemptive suffering. When we suffer for the benefit of some other person, we will experience spiritual growth, and that is rewarded with the feeling of joy. There are several common scenarios where suffering is redemptive. The most common opportunity, but one rarely carried out, occurs when someone is oppressed or exploited and has enough love in his heart to show the oppressors the harm being done to him, giving the oppressors the opportunity to see themselves as they really are and to make amends. In this way, the oppressed show both mercy and forgiveness to their oppressors as Jesus Himself did. If we suffer with Christ, we will also be glorified with Him (Rom. 8:17).

Another common scenario, one slightly easier to carry out, unfolds when we visit suffering loved ones, despite the pain it gives us to see them in this state. Our presence and support make the loved patients feel wanted and important, which reduces their suffering. In this way, we share in a loved one's suffering. By replacing some of the patient's suffering with our own, we show that we can practice self-giving love. This will be discussed in more detail in the third section.

Now, a person can demonstrate redemptive suffering in many ways. The basic criteria are to be willing to suffer as Jesus did, for the benefit of others, and to be willing to carry out our role in God's plan. There are the long-acknowledged examples of the Christian martyrs, who for love of God would not apostatize, even if their decision meant death. It does not have to be this way, though. St. Maximilian Kolbe took the place of a married man picked at random in the Nazi death camp at Auschwitz to be starved to death. This is a very strong example of suffering death for the benefit of another person, in this case a man that St. Maximilian did not even know.[29]

If we have unexplained suffering, we should offer it up to the Lord, showing our willingness to suffer to help bring God's plan to fruition. And at its heart, our reason for offering our suffering up to God is simple: we believe the suffering we endure is for the benefit of someone, whether we can link it to a person we know or not, or simply a way to show our love for God. This is itself a sign of faith that our suffering has a purpose, and that realization can bring joy, which is a sign of spiritual growth.

If we are open to His grace in our life, God uses these four tasks to bring each of us from sin to salvation. Some people experience all of this and are never converted, because they have closed their minds to the existence of God and, thus, they cannot see His work in their lives. If they are ruthless enough, they will exploit others to gain material wealth, only to be surprised that even the greatest wealth does not satisfy their need for God and their true purpose—nor does it stave off suffering, because God will continually reach out to them through the four tasks. They will attempt to ignore this suffering, perhaps by anesthetizing themselves with drugs and alcohol, perhaps by finding diversions like sex, fine foods, or exotic travel, but the emptiness of such a life will always be with them, no matter what surface images they project to others. Many of these people will fool themselves into thinking they are self-sufficient and do not need God, a false premise proven deficient by terminal suffering and death, experiences no one can avoid, regardless of their wealth, fame, or power.

Others have low expectations for themselves and will set peace and comfort as their primary goals in life. These individuals will gear all their beliefs and actions toward those goals, a choice that ultimately leaves their spiritual side greatly compromised by their lack of effort in using God's gifts for their intended purposes. They will also deal with an internal sense that they are not fulfilling their purpose. Instead, they will spend their lives seeking satisfaction in material goods and leisure activities that can never take the place of God. Cursing the suffering in their lives, they never realize that it is God reaching out to them in love, making their bad choices uncomfortable so they choose better alternatives.

In our own lives, we will suffer for a variety of reasons, all of which can drive us to love completely and unconditionally in some way if we heed their messages. Sometimes the suffering is in direct response to something we have done; this is to teach us self-love. Eat too much, we feel sick. Drink too much, we might get a hangover. Steal something from the grocery store, we might be arrested. At other times we may suffer for things that other people have done. If we can find it in our hearts to forgive them and to show them the harm they caused, it is redemptive for us, the victims. If the perpetrators come to realize that their actions are evil, those who repent can be saved. Sometimes possessions and people will be taken away from us because they have become distractions on our way to holiness. Sometimes we may suffer solely for the benefit of others. I think this tends to happen mostly to the righteous, who can be counted on to keep the faith in times of trouble, inspiring others who are undergoing similar hardships, and who will appreciate the spiritual opportunity that redemptive suffering provides.

It was through the redemptive suffering of Christ that man's salvation was made possible (CCC 613). Of course, those who lack strong faith in the love of God and the promises of Christ may have trouble grasping redemptive suffering because it often sacrifices the temporal goods they desire for goods they cannot see that will lead to a salvation they do not recognize or even believe exists. But the truth is, redemptive suffering reveals how much value God places on our union with Him, which He knows is the only thing that can truly satisfy us, far above the things that give us temporal solace. Thus, He will often use suffering to make us see the idols in our lives that distract us from our true missions.

The bottom line is that our Creator forces us to trust Him if we want to be with Him. When trying to understand the suffering in our lives, it is incredibly important to assess how the suffering might be purifying, redirecting, or redeeming, consistent with the perspective that God is good and wants nothing more than our return to Him in love. Every suffering event is teaching us to love ourselves, God, or our neighbors more profoundly. When we willingly suffer for the benefit of another and for the completion of God's plan, we are demonstrating redemptive love, the culmination of our journey to holiness. To do so is to love as God loves, which is to share in the divine nature.

Chapter 6

Rethinking Dying and Terminal Suffering

Linking death directly with suffering, we have the process of dying. Death never changes—it marks the end of mortal life and the beginning of the afterlife. Dying, however, has changed substantially over the last few decades as a consequence of medical and social advances, particularly in the highest economic countries. Most people today have an extended dying period, which gives them more time to prepare themselves and their survivors for their death, but it also extends their suffering and results in more people with dementia. In the United States, six million people currently have Alzheimer's, with the number expected to double by 2040 as the population ages.[30]

Unexpected deaths are fairly rare in modern, industrialized societies because the medical community has good diagnostic tools that can highlight threats to life so the patient is forewarned.

---

[30] Laurie McGinley, "Life under a Cloud for People with Down Syndrome: Many with Genetic Condition Develop Alzheimer's, and They Are Pushing for More Treatments," *Washington Post*, April 12, 2022, A4.

Dying without Fear

High-income countries have government programs and charities to feed, house, clothe, and provide medical care for most of those that need support, and they have developed immune system enhancements that make dying of a contagious disease relatively rare. Enhanced safety standards and protocols, coupled with medical advances, have reduced deaths from injury to less than 6 percent of total deaths. What is left is noncontagious diseases—the body breaking down from age and wear and tear. This is the fate of anyone who survives the other sicknesses and injuries. In the highest income economies, 86 percent of the population now die of noncontagious diseases, mostly cancer and critical organ failure.[31] The net result is that the vast majority of these people would know they are dying prior to death, although people do occasionally die unexpectedly from cardiac arrest and stroke.

An unexpected death is very hard on the survivors, and it does not leave the person much time to reconcile with God. To guard against unexpected death, a person would have to be very diligent about staying in the state of grace. This is not as true for the people with terminal diagnoses who know approximately when they will die. They have the opportunity to reconcile sacramentally with God just before death if they have committed any mortal sin. But no matter the conditions we die under, if we find ourselves at least in Purgatory, assured of eternal happiness after our purification, we will have to consider it a good death. If, on the other hand, we left a great legacy of fame, fortune, and power, and died in

[31] "Global Health Estimates 2019: Estimated Deaths by Cause and Region, 2000 and 2019," World Health Organization, https://cdn.who.int/media/docs/default-source/gho-documents/global-health-estimates/ghe2019_cod_wbincome_2000_201933383745-a750-4d94-8491-fb209dcece6f_7c1ac8d4-d425-4deb-8a12-1dc26c293e80.xlsx?sfvrsn=e7bafa8_9.

the arms of admiring friends and relatives but ended up in Hell, permanently separated from God, our life and death would have to be considered failures.

The terminally ill have the same five needs as anyone else:

* their physical pain
* uncertainty about their medical prognosis
* concern about their purpose in life
* concern about their social status
* concern about what will happen after they die (their spiritual status)

But what makes the five needs different for the terminally is that when people first learn they have a terminal disease, and thus a limited time to live, they can experience intense shock because their illness puts all five needs in doubt.

All humans (indeed, all creatures) are born with the desire for self-preservation (CCC 2281). This most powerful natural instinct, an important recognition of the value of life, is the underlying driver of all the virtues. It reminds us that God is the owner of our lives and that we are merely stewards, tasked with using our lives for the glory of God and the salvation of our souls until God calls us home (CCC 2280). Our desire for self-preservation drives us to love of self and is manifested in the fear of death. Indeed, it is always with us at some level. We naturally evaluate every situation to see if our lives are threatened, whether consciously or subconsciously, and our desire to stay alive makes us cautious around things or situations that can kill us. In fact, the more fragile and exposed we think we are, the greater our tendency to cling to those things that make us feel safe, the greater our inclination to dread uncertainty. We are slaves to death because our every action must consider how to avoid it and preserve our lives. We defeat death when we cease to fear it.

Some maintain that we are dying from the day we are born, but that is only true from the standpoint that we know we will die. Dying is the process by which the soul leaves the body, which only happens when the body is unable to be sustained. The United States Conference of Catholic Bishops, in its *Ethical and Religious Directives for Catholic Health Care Services*, warns that "what is hardest to face is the process of dying itself, especially the dependency, the helplessness, and the pain that so often accompany terminal illness."[32]

The reasons the bishops cite are interesting because, while those who do not know or understand the motivations of our loving God certainly do experience these elements as negatives, they are all part of God calling us home to eternal happiness, the greatest good.

Fear of dependency is one of the main reasons people in Oregon turn to physician-assisted suicide,[33] but to be dependent on someone is to be open to accepting their love. Those afraid of dependency are either concerned that they will not be loved by anyone and will be left uncared for, or they just shun the help of others, turning away their love, which is detrimental to both parties. One of the main benefits of terminal suffering is to teach us all that we are dependent on God, and if we cannot accept that, we will not be happy in His Kingdom, where God provides all we need.

[32] USCCB, *Ethical and Religious Directives for Catholic Health Care Services*, 6th ed. (Washington, D.C.: USCCB, 2018), 19, https://www.usccb.org/about/doctrine/ethical-and-religious-directives/upload/ethical-religious-directives-catholic-health-service-sixth-edition-2016-06.pdf.

[33] Angela Morrow, "Reasons for Requesting Physician-Assisted Suicide" *Very Well Health*, March 23, 2020, https://www.verywell-health.com/reasons-for-seeking-physician-assisted-suicide-1132378.

Those feeling helpless—the feeling St. Paul no doubt had when God knocked him off his horse on the road to Damascus (Acts 9:1–8)—are being called to align themselves with God with overwhelming force. It is the harsher way to experience the second task of suffering for those who have not yet turned to God, who can solve all problems. This feeling of helplessness is an invitation from God to approach Him. It is a step beyond dependency to feel that you cannot be helped. This is God showing you the limitations of this world and of medical science and causing you to seek Him, who alone can heal you and make you whole in His Kingdom.

Pain is the feeling of suffering that comes with a lack of bodily integrity. It is God telling us we have a problem, and if it is severe enough, it will convince us that living on earth is untenable and will push us toward pursuing spiritual growth and new life in the new heavens and the new earth after Judgment Day instead of trying to extend our lives on earth.

The Church recognizes that different people will react very differently to a life-threatening disease. In the Church's experience, very often people will turn to God because of the ordeal, which is the point. But some will revolt against God because of the suffering.

The Church explains her experience in the *Catechism* as follows:

Illness and suffering have always been among the gravest problems confronted in human life. In illness, man experiences his powerlessness, his limitations, and his finitude. Every illness can make us glimpse death. Illness can lead to anguish, self-absorption, sometimes even despair and revolt against God. It can also make a person more mature, helping him discern in his life what is not essential so that he can turn toward that which is. Very often illness provokes a search for God and a return to him. (CCC 1500–1501)

In this very important paragraph, the Church acknowledges that suffering is a catalyst for conversion but also notes that suffering can make some people resent and revolt against God. It does not speculate on what makes people react differently, but I think it clearly is driven by what the person perceives is God's intention toward him and what that person believes about suffering and death. It would seem quite natural for a person who is suffering without explanation to resent it and to revolt against the person causing it. It takes a higher degree of spiritual maturity and a firm belief in the goodness of God to look past the discomfort and comprehend how a loving God can use this suffering to perfect, protect, and redirect us to joy and eternal life.

This difference in perspective changes everything. The acclaimed author and disability advocate Nancy Mairs is an excellent case study for this because she experienced both the positive and negative aspects. Mairs was twenty-nine and had just entered graduate school to study creative writing when she was diagnosed with MS (multiple sclerosis), a degenerative, chronic condition that normally does not result in death directly but in rare cases can be fatal or could significantly affect quality of life and weaken the person so that she dies of a secondary cause.[34] Mairs did not take the diagnosis well, leaving her husband and two small children, having a series of affairs, and ultimately attempting suicide.[35]

---

[34] "What Is Multiple Sclerosis," Johns Hopkins Medicine, https://www.hopkinsmedicine.org/health/conditions-and-diseases/multiple-sclerosis-ms.

[35] Nancy L. Eiesland, *The Disabled God: Toward a Liberatory Theology of Disability* (Nashville: Abingdon Press, 1994), 40–43.

After a year of depression and roaming, Mairs recognized that her body was degrading slower than anticipated. Now relooking at her situation with greater maturity, Mairs realized that she could still do many of her normal activities and returned to the life she had been leading pre-diagnosis. She also slowly became aware of her body and its unity with her soul. She found God and converted to Catholicism. With this conversion came an understanding of her own need for mercy, as well as an acceptance of suffering and her eventual death. She began writing as a "crippled woman," finding a new powerful purpose for her life that propelled her to a much larger audience than she had previously.[36] She wrote of her life and her illness-driven limitations unflinchingly and with a comedic wit in a series of memoirs that included *Remembering the Bone House: An Erotics of Place and Space* (1989), *Carnal Acts* (1990), *Voice Lessons: On Becoming a (Woman) Writer* (1994), and *Waist-High in the World: A Life among the Nondisabled* (1996). Interspersed with these were two other memoirs, *Ordinary Time: Cycles in Marriage, Faith and Renewal* (1993) and *A Dynamic God: Living an Unconventional Catholic Faith* (2007), in which she described her conversion to Roman Catholicism, and the ways her newfound faith shaped her mental world and her attitude toward suffering, death, and the social fabric. "To view your life as blessed does not require you to deny your pain," she wrote in the introduction to *Carnal Acts*. "It simply demands a more complicated vision, one in which a condition or event is not either good or bad but is, rather, both good and bad, not sequentially but simultaneously. In my experience, the more such ambivalences you can hold in your head, the better off you are, intellectually and emotionally." As a measure of her influence

---

[36] Ibid., 43–46.

and notoriety, most of this information comes from a glowing obituary in the *New York Times*.[37]

It takes a lot to separate the soul from the body. Dying is mostly accomplished through disease, with catastrophic injury the only other choice. Disease, broadly taken, comes from three sources. The first results from the body not being given its essential needs, from oxygen and food and water to specific vitamins and minerals. The second is due to a lack of immunity against microbial and viral attack—in other words, contagious diseases. The third and final type of illness is bodily breakdown, generally categorized as noncontagious diseases, from major organ failures, cancers, or diseases of the brain such as Parkinson's and Alzheimer's. It hurts to die because our sense of suffering is enacted when we are missing some required good that threatens our existence, precisely what is happening when we die. And because what actually kills us is, by definition, our greatest threat, suffering is most severe at the end of life.

Not everyone experiences terminal suffering. Some die of disease or injury before their bodies break down. Industrialized countries all have social programs to feed the poor, and the medical community has developed drugs and protocols that have proven effective in raising immunity and controlling infectious diseases. This means that in the industrialized world, the vast majority of people will survive injuries, overcome infectious diseases, and avoid starvation, eventually going on to die after age seventy, when their bodies break down. In lower income countries, only about a third

---

[37] William Grimes, "Nancy Mairs, Who Wrote about Her Mental Illness and Multiple Sclerosis, Dies at 73," *New York Times*, December 8, 2016, A-29, https://www.nytimes.com/2016/12/07/books/nancy-mairs-dead-author.html.

of people will make it that far, with infections killing more than half of the population.[38]

In industrialized economies, over 86 percent of the people die of some form of bodily breakdown, usually cancer or the functional decay of the essential organs.[39] This is not limited to the very old, although that is the expected reality for most people. Some people have conditions that weaken the body, leading to terminal illnesses and suffering at younger ages, some even as infants. For instance, Tay-Sachs disease, a rare, inherited lipid metabolism disorder, causes too much of a fatty substance to build up in the brain, a process that begins in the womb. Affected children experience a form of terminal suffering beginning at about six months of age, when they have progressive loss of mental ability, blindness, deafness, seizures, difficulty swallowing, and dementia, leading to death by age five, even with the best of care.[40]

Suffering itself is important to the dying process. It makes the possibility of dying real and thus stands as a warning prior to death. This advance warning serves the sufferer in several ways. First, terminal suffering is harsh enough that it becomes clear we are dying and that nothing we can do will stop it. This sense that we are mortal and not in control of our own destiny is shocking and terrifying at the same time. In many, if not most, cases, the person will react by contemplating his life—what has been important in it and what has been missing. The Church's experience is that many will search for and find God at this point, when

[38] World Health Organization, Global Health Estimates 2016, HI table. https://www.who.int/data/global-health-estimates.

[39] Ibid.

[40] "Tay-Sachs Disease," Genetic and Rare Diseases Information Center, National Institutes of Health, https://rarediseases.info.nih.gov/diseases/7737/tay-sachs-disease.

there is still time to reconcile with Him (CCC 1501). Terminal suffering also gives us the impetus to put our affairs in order and to reconcile with anyone we have become estranged from for any reason. It allows us to work on anything we wish to leave as a legacy. Finally, terminal suffering makes it clear that eternal life is not tenable or desirable in our current condition, thus making the transition that is death much easier to embrace and making it easier for our loved ones to accept our deaths as a sign of God's love and mercy.

Even for those of us who have been diagnosed with a terminal disease, the diagnosis lacks credibility without suffering to support it. I had a congenital heart defect that required open heart surgery twice. The first surgery, in 1965, was nearly fatal—my heart stopped twice on the operating table—and failed to fix the underlying problem. During the second operation, in 1977, they successfully patched the septal defect that was preventing my blood from carrying sufficient oxygen to my body for it to run efficiently. The euphoria I felt as I rode my bike around the block for the first time was tempered somewhat by the fact that my left arm was paralyzed in the surgery. Fortunately, the pinched nerve in my spine healed itself in six weeks, so I entered my senior year in high school feeling pretty good about myself—until someone told me that people with heart conditions like mine had life expectancies of about fifty-two years.

That number stood in the back of my mind for decades, but I never felt worried enough to take any specific action, because it never caused me much pain. And now that I have blown ten years past that mark, I realize the diagnosis was obviously meaningless and wonder why anyone would tell a seventeen-year-old that—although I do also concede that my seventeen-year-old self would probably have dismissed any nuanced thought about probabilities and inability to read the future as worthless information and considered what was an estimate as an undisputed fact.

The second time I was told I had a potentially fatal disease was when I was forty-two, and that came after twenty-five years of good health, or so I thought, until I came home from a family trip to California in 2002 to find sixteen urgent messages from my doctor on the answering machine, one for every day we were gone. I had been diagnosed with hepatitis C after a routine blood check before taking a statin drug to control a hereditary cholesterol problem. I was told it could be potentially fatal but that fortunately there was a new ribavirin-interferon drug protocol that was successful in resolving the virus in a high percentage of cases like mine. I never felt my life threatened by hepatitis C because, frankly, I never felt any symptoms. In fact, it showed up at the time of my life that I felt the healthiest I had ever been. That healthy period came to a screeching halt, however, because the drug protocol had very harsh side effects. I spent the next six months with severe nausea, headaches, and tremors, but it did resolve the hepatitis.

Ironically, the third time I was diagnosed with a potentially fatal disease, the doctor did not actually tell me that. What he said was this: "You have Parkinson's disease, but do not think of it as a death sentence. You still will have five to ten years of functionality, and we're working hard for a cure, so you never know." The fact that he introduced it that way made me think it might actually be a death sentence, so I immediately went home and looked up Parkinson's online to see what I was up against. It was daunting, as I expected. While it does not directly kill, it does cause both physical and mental degradation to the point where one is bedridden and totally dependent on others and susceptible to other maladies, which will be shown as the cause of death. Seventy percent of Parkinson's patients die of pneumonia.[41] My current doctor has told me to plan on two to three years of functioning at my current levels but also took the opportunity to warn me that if I stop doing so, I will rapidly degrade. I appreciated his bluntness because it gave me an opportunity to plan for the future, and the impetus to keep working through the challenges of Parkinson's at a time when it is becoming harder and harder to do so.

The physical degradation from Parkinson's is undeniable and increasingly problematic. This is a much different experience than with my previous two terminal diagnoses. With them, I was never limited. I now have a hard time getting up from a chair and into and out of bed. One of the real annoyances is my lack of general strength. It is hard to open bottles and even bags of chips. Whereas a year ago I was able to build a large two-tier deck on the back of my house, this week I struggled to build a few simple benches. It was difficult for me to pull the trigger on the electric drill, and getting up from the ground was a major effort. And because I now lack the strength and agility to play any sports, my weight has ballooned. Fortunately, so far, I am not degrading mentally, but I know that time is coming. The question is, will I be able to perceive it when it is here? This time, it feels like a fatal disease.

I do find myself discerning what is important in life and what I should be doing in my limited, remaining productive period. Writing this book seems to be the way God is pointing me—I feel compelled to complete it, and I rarely feel the symptoms of Parkinson's while writing it. I do not feel like death is knocking at the door, but I do sense it is coming. I do not fear it; God has seen to that by sending me on this journey, for which I am most grateful. Hopefully, you, who are on this journey with me, come to feel the same way.

This realization that I have a terminal disease took on new relevancy in October 2022 as this book was going into editing, because I had brain surgery the week before we began the editing process. Deep brain stimulation (DBS), to be precise. It is the last step of treatment for Parkinson's disease and is only given after all medical (read drug) therapies have been tried and are no longer effective. As brain surgeries go, it is routine; over 150,000 Parkinson's patients have had it to date. In concept it is similar to a heart's pacemaker.

But it is still brain surgery, with finite risks of death and strokes, so part of my prep was to get Anointing of the Sick, the sacrament of the Catholic Church given to those in danger of death from sickness or old age to provide the graces of strengthening, peace, and courage to face what is ahead. The anointing is clearly pointing to the celestial kingdom, uniting our suffering to that of Christ while promising physical healing only if it is critical to the salvation of souls. It is scary to contemplate that this is the last possible treatment for Parkinson's and from here it is all downhill, in addition to the reality that I was allowing a doctor to drill holes into my head, so the graces present in the sacrament were appropriate and desired.

DBS is typically done in two stages. In the first stage, the task is to embed the electrodes into the brain. It takes five to six hours and is by far the most delicate and scary part of the surgery. It is also highly interactive, depending on the patient to accurately articulate what they can see, hear, and feel during the critical placement of the electrodes into the brain. For instance, I felt that they were suppressing my heartbeat with one placement, which they immediately corrected. They sent me to a neuropsychologist for four hours of extensive testing of my mental acuity a week before the procedure to establish a baseline and to ensure that I was not suffering from depression or dementia and could give them responses that they were sure were accurate.

The setup for the first stage is interesting. They put me out in order to shave my head and screw a steel frame to it. Then they woke me up, and from then on I felt like part of the surgical team, although I was invested a little more than the rest of them. It was a strange feeling when they told me it was going to be loud while they drilled the nickel-sized holes in my skull. I was just hoping they stopped in time to not hit the actual brain. The doctor had predetermined, with an MRI, target locations for the electrodes. They then adjusted the final placement of the electrodes through their interaction with me. They knew by my responses whether they were in the optimum place or not: sometimes by judging my ability to follow a finger, sometimes by checking my ability to count the fingers they held up, sometimes by repeating phrases they said. Ironically, they correct based on errors, so if you would have made these errors anyway, you provide false information. The more mentally capable and alert you are, the better your results are likely to be.

The second stage is done on an outpatient basis under general anesthesia. It only took the doctor about an hour to place the pulse generator under my collarbone and feed wires under my skin to attach to the leads. They will wait two weeks for the brain to heal, and then they will take out the stitches and staples—arranged like two train tracks running parallel across my shaved scalp—and program the system, at which point I will see the result of my gamble. The surgical team was confident and very complimentary about the quality of my responses in the first stage of the surgery, and so they felt I would be very pleased with the quality of life the treatment offers for five years or more.

The gamble was whether to pull the trigger on the last resort for enhanced quality of life with Parkinson's, and whether to do it before completing a series of events that are important for me and my family, knowing that there existed a small but real chance I would not survive the surgery. These events included hosting my children at home for Thanksgiving, then going on a cruise in Australia and New Zealand with my wife over Christmas and New Year's Day. I would get back just in time to teach nursing ethics in the spring semester at the Catholic University of America. A couple of days after the final exams, my son Dan will marry his college sweetheart, Carly Bibber, which will be a joyous family event. As it turns out, it was the right choice because now I will likely be able to enjoy these experiences with better health. Further, I will be able to support the rollout of this book, *Dying without Fear*, which Sophia Press is expected to release in June 2023.

No one wants to get a diagnosis of a potentially fatal disease. While everyone knows intellectually that they are going to die, an actual diagnosis of a fatal disease brings that reality into sharper focus. But to get such a diagnosis is actually a blessing because it allows you to plan what time you have left and to reconcile with God and anyone on earth you're estranged from. I took care to do this before my brain surgery, which was potentially fatal. For me, it also provides a sense of urgency to share what I've learned in all the venues available to me while I still can.

Not everyone gets such a diagnosis, however, because it is as difficult a message to give to someone as it is to receive, especially in a medical culture that has come to believe death is a failure of medicine. Many doctors, recognizing their own limitations, are hesitant to come out and say, "You are going to die," preferring to soften the blow with talks of potential cures and new exploratory procedures that give the patient hope, as was the case with my New York neurologist. This is not unwarranted, because after all there are 16.9 million cancer survivors in the United States alone,[42] most of whom had a terminal diagnosis. However, medicine does have its limits, and no one escapes death. It is ethically incumbent on medical professionals to give the best information they have on the patient's prognosis to allow the patient to make the appropriate plans for both death and what comes after that. In retrospect, perhaps that is why someone told me at seventeen of my decreased life expectancy, although they were obviously in error.

There are a great number of ways to die, and people have different viewpoints on how they want to depart this life and what kind of death they want. Some active military types wish to go down in a blaze of glory. Others want no drama at all, preferring to pass away in their sleep. Still others wish to die in the company of loved ones in a comfortable place. This is probably the biggest group, but for it to happen, you must have a warning that God is going to call you home. This only occurs for those with a terminal illness who have undergone some level of terminal suffering to let them know that the time for death is upon them.

Thomas Aquinas taught that this bodily breakdown was a direct impact of the Fall, noting that original justice would have placed the body under the control of the soul, keeping the body from breaking down.[43] It is not clear that medical science has a better answer. Dying of bodily breakdown is generally much slower and

---

[42] "Cancer Statistics," National Cancer institute, National Institutes of Health, September 25, 2020, https://www.cancer.gov/about-cancer/understanding/statistics.

[43] *ST* I, q. 95, art. 1.

more painful than dying of injury or infection. These are important attributes because the pain prepares the sufferer for death and the delay gives the sufferer and the survivors time to do that preparation. This is a significant advantage over unexpected deaths resulting from other causes.

For instance, a person who is unexpectedly hit by a bus and dies has no warning to get absolution for his sins and to exit the world in the state of grace. Granted, the Church warns people to visit the confessional at least once per month to stay in the state of grace in case of an unexpected death, but that advice is often ignored. Further, the person killed by the bus has no warning or impetus to reconcile with anyone he is estranged from or to train his survivors in what he was doing, leaving a bigger hole in their lives than the person whose body is breaking down and can plan accordingly. Again, it is granted that a supremely organized person could keep those around him trained in relevant matters so his legacy could be passed on even in the event of a tragic, unexpected death, but few are that organized and that motivated.

In truth, unexpected death is very hard on the survivors. They are faced with an immediate emotional void and possible regrets concerning unresolved issues. They must also deal with logistics hurdles concerning responsibilities you may have had, responsibilities no one knows about or how to accomplish. Some may be dependent on you and are now faced with replacing that dependency "on the fly." These are all issues that can be resolved if you know you are dying.

At the same time, harsh end-of-life suffering makes it abundantly clear that living forever in this world is untenable and undesirable—for both the suffering individuals and those around them. This serves as a motivator for the faithful to progress in their spiritual life and as a warning, to those who are not, of the fallacy of trying to live forever on earth. This suffering also makes it far easier for their loved ones to accept their deaths and their own sense of loss. Most of them will see it as a mercy from God, which it is.

This was definitely the case with my mother, Dolly Chaloux, who suffered tremendously the last few years of her life and died at the age of ninety the week I wrote this. As much as we loved her, all six of her children knew her quality of life was abysmal the last few years as she suffered with dementia, and we were relieved for her when she was called home on Mother's Day 2022.

In her case, she had been in hospice for fourteen months and exhibited all the signs of advanced dementia: she could no longer verbally communicate, she could not move any of her limbs, and in the last week she could no longer swallow. She had lost maybe fifty pounds by this time and was extremely thin. One day a tooth fell out. On Saturday morning, May 7, the hospice nurse told me that she would not live beyond seventy-two hours. This was a great kindness by the hospice nurse because it allowed us to plan for our mother's passing. She had been given the sacrament of Anointing of the Sick—Last Rites—on Thursday night (and for the third or fourth time), so we felt comfortable that we had met her spiritual needs. Four of her six children lived locally, so we set up a schedule to ensure my mother would not die alone.

On Sunday, May 8 (Mother's Day), I had the second shift, from 11:00 a.m. to 1:00 p.m. When I arrived, my mother was having a very hard time breathing, so it was clear she did not have much time left. My sister Sandra and her husband, Tom, who had the first shift, said their goodbyes and left me alone with my dying mother, who had some fluid in her lungs, which you could hear with every breath. I tried to talk to her, but she was clearly fully occupied just trying to breathe. I then sent a text out to the family and set up a Zoom call, which allowed the two out-of-town siblings, Janet and Mike, to say their goodbyes; my brother Rich, who had the fourth shift at 3:00, logged in as well. Rich sent me a compendium of prayers for the dying, which I said, along with a Rosary, for my mom, while waiting for the others to join. When they joined the Zoom call, I explained the situation and then put the screen in front of my mother so they could each say their goodbyes. I noticed a tear in my mother's eye, so I tried to assure her that everything would be okay.

It was about this time that my youngest sister, Maria, and her fiancé, David, arrived to relieve me. They took positions by the hospital bed and began to say their goodbyes as I packed up to leave. I said what was to be my last goodbye and walked out the door. I had second thoughts about leaving and came back and said one last goodbye, then walked out. I had just gotten out of the building and into the car when my brother Rich called me and asked where I was. I told him I had just gotten into the car, and he told me to look at my text messages. My sister Maria had texted that my mom had stopped breathing. I went back in, and she said that my mom had passed seconds after I left the room. She felt that my mother had been holding on until she saw her, the sixth and final child to visit, at least remotely, that day.

While we all thought it meaningful that she passed on Mother's Day, Rich found some additional consolation in that May 8 is also the feast of the Apparition of St. Michael the Archangel, to whom he has a special devotion. According to the *Catholic Encyclopedia*, among the four traditional offices (or roles) of St. Michael is escorting the faithful to heaven, protecting them from the evil one, at the hour of death.[44]

---

[44] Frederick Holweck, "St. Michael the Archangel," *The Catholic Encyclopedia*, vol. 10 (New York: Robert Appleton Company, 1911), http://www.newadvent.org/cathen/10275b.htm.

It is easy to feel inadequate in these situations. I doubt that I said anything of great importance to my mother on that last day. I am not sure I could have. I suspect the fact that she saw all six of her children in her last hour or two was the most important gift we could give her, other than the sacraments. And this gift of our presence was only possible because she had experienced a terminal diagnosis and terminal suffering so that we knew when to be there and when to get the sacraments.

Some would question whether the send-off was worth the suffering, but remember, too, the effect on the survivors. Because of that suffering, we all were prepared emotionally for her death, knowing full well that her body had completely given out and that she had pushed it as far as it would go in her ninety years. This is not to say we are not grieving and do not feel the loss. We are and we do, three weeks after the event. This sorrow and this feeling of loss are unavoidable when a close relative passes, whether it be parent, spouse, or child — they play such a big part in our lives that they *have* to be missed. Nevertheless, it would be far worse if we did not have the warning and the suffering to show us that it was indeed time for them to move on to the next world.

Perhaps the scariest part of dying for many people is that they will end their life with Alzheimer's disease or some other form of dementia, like my mother did. This disease, which is marked by severe memory loss, affects mostly the very old, who have survived everything else. The average age of first diagnosis of Alzheimer's disease for the "normal" population is eighty, but for those with Down syndrome, whose bodies break down much earlier, the age of first diagnosis is fifty-four.[45] As discussed earlier, Tay-Sachs victims will have dementia before the age of five. Combined, more

[45] McGinley, "Life under a Cloud," A-1, A-4.

than 96 percent of those who die from Alzheimer's are beyond seventy years old. Indeed, as other diseases have been cured, the prevalence of dementia has increased, killing more people in the industrialized world in recent years than all injuries combined.[46] Dementia can be hard on caregivers because dementia patients lose the ability to communicate verbally and often compensate with repetitive questioning, crying, agitation, wandering, and, at times, even physical violence against themselves and others.[47] Interestingly, there is a debate between sociologists and the medical community about whether dementia is a disease or simply a normal stage in the dying process.[48] While it is true that not every senior citizen is senile, it is equally true that few if any people have dementia as youths without some other contributing factors that bring on terminal suffering earlier. From my vantage point and experience, people degrade at different times, in different ways, and at different rates, but if you live long enough, you will eventually experience it. It is not something that you "catch"—it is just an aspect of our individual physiologies that, sooner or later, our mortal bodies give out.

Cynically, the debate about Alzheimer's being a disease or a normal part of the aging process is about research grants: medicine gets funding for curing diseases, social sciences get funding for dealing with life cycle issues. But it has greater ramifications than research funding—it affects how dementia patients are treated. If Alzheimer's is a disease, symptoms are treated with drugs, mostly sedatives, to calm the clinical behavior and make

[46] World Health Organization, Global Health Estimates 2019, HI table, https://www.who.int/data/global-health-estimates.

[47] Athena McLean, *The Person in Dementia: A Study of Nursing Home Care in the U.S.* (Ontario, CA: Broadview Press, 2007), 22.

[48] Ibid., 29.

the demented patient compliant. On the other hand, if this is considered a sociology concern, caregivers will look to decipher the clinical behavior as a mother diagnoses the cries of her infant child, going through a checklist of needs (cold, hungry, thirsty, bored, frustrated or angry about their care) to determine what the demented patient is trying to express. The difference between treating dementia like a disease or treating dementia patients as normal dying people is stark. Diseases are treated with drugs; people are treated with care.

Often, the demented elders remember vividly the epic stories of their past and can continue to share detailed memories long after they lost the ability to remember what they had for breakfast. Even after they have lost the ability to communicate verbally, the habits formed over a lifetime continue as reminders of what they felt was important and what distinguished them from others. Dementia patients also have moments of lucidity, which fade over time, forming a slow goodbye that allows everyone to get comfortable with the eventual end. When death comes, most people will concede that it is a blessing that dementia patients are moving on to another existence where they will be fully capable again.

Although many believe that loss of memory is a loss of self, this is clearly not the case. Dementia still allows people to practice through habit those skills that they know well. For example, my uncle Andy Chaloux, who has severe Alzheimer's disease and can no longer speak or recognize close relatives, recently scored a hole in one and shot under his age (eighty-seven) in golf.[49] He is an avid

---

[49] Andrew Johnson Golf Club, "We would like to congratulate Andy Chaloux today," Facebook, July 30, 2021, https://www.facebook.com/ajgolfclub/posts/we-would-like-to-congratulate-andy-chaloux-today-for-his-amazing-hole-in-one-tod/4583117918393623/.

and accomplished golfer, having shot his age or lower — the goal of senior golfers — over one hundred times prior to the age of eighty, so he had built up muscle memory for the mechanics of his stroke that did not rely on short-term memory.[50] And he is not alone in continuing to excel in his passion despite dementia. Other people have demonstrated the ability to weave, groom themselves, and even read the Torah long after they had lost their memories.[51]

Beyond this, we also hear accounts of those with dementia that give rise to the thought that they may have more agency than they are given credit for. In his book *Dementia*, John Swinton, Scottish theologian and advocate for the demented, explains the case of an elderly woman with dementia, who was found in an agitated state, pacing the corridors of her elder-care facility repeating the word *God* over and over, annoying both the staff and the other residents. A particularly enlightened nurse walked alongside her for a while and then, in a flash of inspiration, asked the woman if she was afraid of forgetting God. When the elderly woman emphatically answered in the affirmative, the nurse told her, "You know, even if you should forget God, He will not forget you. He has promised that." The old woman, thus assured of God's continued love, became peaceful.[52]

The implications of this exchange are profound. We do not know anything about the elderly woman's background except that

[50] Wayne Philips, "Local Golfer Has Shot His Age or Lower 100 Times" *Greeneville Sun*, October 13, 2013, https://www.greenev-illesun.com/sports/local-golfer-has-shot-his-age-or-lower-100-times/article_a7b0da7f-a7be-55da-81d9-5414480dddf3.html.

[51] Michael Banner, *The Ethics of Everyday Life* (Oxford: Oxford University Press, 2014), 130.

[52] John Swinton, *Dementia: Living in the Memories of God* (Grand Rapids, MI: Eerdmans, 2012), 196–197.

she had severe dementia. Yet she was worried about the same thing that millions of other sufferers ask themselves as death approaches: "Did God forget about me?"

Perhaps we are looking at dementia all wrong. What if this is God's way of easing us into death and is a great kindness? Maybe it is not related to age at all but to the reality that perhaps short-term memory loss is just another step in the breakdown of bodily processes. After all, it seems to be accelerated in Down syndrome patients and even Tay-Sachs patients consistent with their bodily breakdowns. Indeed, the final stages of dementia involve complete breakdown of the body's systems. The late stages of dementia also include the inability to move one's body and, eventually, the loss of one's ability to swallow, which means someone can no longer eat or drink. Death naturally follows after a few days.[53]

The loss of short-term memory greatly reduces functionality but also presumably reduces the ongoing sense of loss by the dying and keeps them from dwelling on the pain resulting from the breakdown of the rest of the body. This is not to suggest that those in the final stages of dementia do not experience pain or recognize the loss, because they clearly do. But they live "in the moment," so perhaps it is easier to take that way. I know that I can be distracted from my own immediate suffering if I am engaged in other activities, like writing this book, so perhaps it is like that for the demented. If they lack short-term memory and are living in the moment, a visitor might be enough to distract them from their pain for a while.

[53] "Caring for a Person With Late-Stage Alzheimer's Disease," National Institute on Aging, National Institutes of Health, May 27, 2021, https://www.nia.nih.gov/health/caring-late-stage-alzheimers-disease.

Interestingly, modern medical care treats pain as the most fundamental illness of the elderly. As part of what is now called palliative care, sedatives are administered to the point that patients are rarely conscious. This is a real challenge for caregivers who want to try to communicate with their demented loved ones, because the medical establishment's priorities for those with dementia are pain control and patient control; as such, medical personnel are not easily persuaded to reduce the dose levels. While physical comfort should certainly be addressed, it is a mistake to treat pain as a pathology, because it is not. Pain is, after all, a warning that you have a pathology that needs to be treated. Silencing the messenger does nothing to solve the root problem. Yes, pain can be debilitating, especially at the end of life, and suppressing it may be necessary so you can get important tasks completed, but sedating a person does not allow this to happen and is thus unproductive.

In truth, I think medical personnel undervalue the need and ability of the demented to say goodbye to their loved ones. I think I would be willing to withstand any level of physical pain to be conversant to the end, though I have not reached that stage. My mother did, but for the last couple months of her life she was sedated so heavily that she was rarely awake and never fully conscious. My brother, who had medical power of attorney, tried several times to get the hospice medical team to back off the sedatives so my mother could get ready to die, but he could not get them to comply, because they were concerned about her pain level. I grant that her pain was extreme, but they favored bodily comfort over caring for her soul, effectively ending her conscious life a few months early to keep her out of pain. This is a trade-off people should consider when writing their advance directives and discussing care with future surrogates—although, as we experienced, surrogates will have a hard time affecting the actual care of their loved ones without a change in the medical community's view of the priorities of healing the body versus the soul. For all the discussion of patient autonomy, medical teams still have considerable power in their facilities, and if you have an advance directive on file that says to aggressively treat pain, then the surrogate is powerless to alter your care.

In its ethical and religious directives, the USCCB recognizes the value of pain relief for the patient but also recognizes the patient's right to consciousness in directive 61, which says in part:

> Patients should be kept as free of pain as possible so that they may die comfortably and with dignity, and in the place where they wish to die. Since a person has the right to prepare for his or her death while fully conscious, he or she should not be deprived of consciousness without a compelling reason.[54]

While it may or may not be true that those with dementia experience some level of relief of temporal suffering because of their condition, it is clearly true that others can benefit spiritually because of it. This is because dementia makes the person dependent on others, who if they answer the call will be providing aid and showing mercy "for one of these least brothers," the critical factor for salvation described by Jesus in His parable of the Last Judgment in Matthew's Gospel (25:31–46).

Dementia typically progresses gradually, allowing both the dying and the caregivers time to adjust to increasing levels of dependency. Dementia patients obviously need to be dependent on others as the condition intensifies. As I will discuss in more detail in the

[54] USCCB, *Ethical and Religious Directives*, no. 61, https://www.usccb.org/resources/ethical-religious-directives-catholic-health-service-sixth-edition-2016-06_1.pdf.

third section, the caregivers will suffer along with their demented patient, both emotionally and, at times, physically. Therefore, both parties suffer for the benefit of the other, which is redemptive if borne willingly out of love for the other and for God and His plan.

Chapter 7

Rethinking Death

Terminal illness naturally leads to death. What most, if not all, people can agree on is that death is the end of mortal life, where the soul is separated from the body, which will decay, and as the Ash Wednesday ritual states, in tribute to God's curse of Adam after the Fall, we return to the dust from which we came (Gen. 3:19). Some people believe this is all that happens. They are probably not reading this book, because they believe they already have the answer to why people die—that it is just fate and that life and death have no higher meaning. Other people are certain that life is not a random occurrence and that everything is done for a reason. They search for that reason in a variety of ways, looking for plausible solutions, ones consistent with their other held beliefs. It is for people like this that I wrote this book.

Life is good precisely *because* we have death. Without death, life as we know it could not exist. After the Fall of Man, our bodies are too fragile for life to be eternal. More importantly, this world is not big enough and does not offer enough stimulation to last for eternity. The super wealthy already experience this. Able to afford anything they want, they soon find that nothing they can buy can bring satisfaction. Indeed, the unhappiest people on earth are probably the spoiled offspring of the wealthy who are given everything they want, thus depriving them of any self-satisfaction at doing something well or having any sense of purpose. This is why we witness so many cases of those who "seem to have it all" anesthetizing themselves with drugs and alcohol. Humans get bored easily; we need new challenges to give our lives purpose and meaning. Granted, some need more stimulation than others, but we all would suffer from extreme boredom if we were not challenged. It is in our makeup because the more we do, materially and spiritually, the more we grow, and as Aquinas says, everything desires its own perfection because it seeks God.[55]

As philosopher Martha Nussbaum points out, what makes things valuable is that they are rare, useful, and can be lost.[56] This is true of human life in general. If it could not be lost, we would value it less. The same goes for time. If it were infinite, we would not value it as we do today.

Finally, there is the practical reality of the current universal design. It is a finite, closed environment, where the organic material must be recycled to bring on new life or merely to let some elements grow. Each new growth of life must come at the expense of other existing living organisms because, in a material world, everything needs to eat. As the human population grows—and without death or a vigorous lock on procreation, there is nothing to stop it from growing—it consumes more and more of the finite organic resources of the earth until at some point there will be nothing left to consume but each other. Since this could not proceed without death, life as we know it could not proceed without death either.

[55] ST I, q. 6, art. 1, resp. to obj. 2.
[56] Martha Nussbaum, The Therapy of Desire (Princeton: Princeton University Press, 2009), 226-233.

The only way a closed system can function is with a very efficient recycling system, or, like a snow globe, nothing can be allowed to change. Therefore, the only way to keep humans from overwhelming the environment without death is if humans could not reproduce, which would of course change life dramatically. There would be no need for two sexes or any families to bond people together. Without family ties and responsibilities, people would likely become even more self-centered than they are today. An eternal life lived alone seems dreadful compared to what we have now, without even considering the inevitable breakdown of the human body and the exhaustion of things of interest to do on earth.

The Church teaches that death is a consequence of sin and that if man did not sin, he would have been immune to death (CCC 413, 418). She also notes that "God did not make death, nor does He rejoice in the destruction of the living" (CCC 413; Wisd. 1:13). This is undoubtedly true. But it also seems clear that God's plan foresaw the sin of Adam and Eve.[57] This is made obvious by the fact that if there were no death, then the evolutionary plan would not function. This is consistent with the concept that God is outside of time and sees all things at once. He did not react to Adam and Eve's sin—He anticipated it with the plan that featured sending the incarnate Son of God to redeem humanity

[57] Adam and Eve acted freely, which God foresaw. Had they not sinned, then the order of the world would be different, since it would be free from suffering and death. This of course raises interesting questions for speculative theology concerning where all the generations of man would live and get the resources. This opens up additional questions of what would have happened if subsequent generations had sinned. The speculations, while interesting are beyond the scope of this book.

through suffering. He set up Heaven, which Jesus opened with His paschal sacrifice, and then, to motivate man to the proper love of self and get him back on the road to eternal life, He gave man the ability to suffer when he was threatened or was doing something harmful to himself. Why? Because God loves us and wants us to join Him forever.

In truth, the wisdom of our Creator shows forth in the institution of death. The Church recognizes that "it was through the devil's envy that death entered the world" (CCC 413; Wisd. 2:24). But it also recognizes that God can bring good out of evil, and indeed He has done so with death. Life possesses more meaning because it can be lost. After all, things that can never be lost, no matter what we do, have very little value to us. Death does limit humans to a finite set of accomplishments because we have a finite amount of time to carry them out. This makes our achievements all the more valued and celebrated when they happen. Human progress is accelerated because death imbues a task with a sense of urgency, the desire to get it done before it is too late. There is not much urgency required or satisfaction gained when you have forever in which to do it. Death also encourages sharing information with future generations so they can carry on our legacies when we are gone. Without death, once the world has been filled, there would be no new generations.

Now, if death is required for the universal plan to work, God needed a specific plan to communicate this and also to make our demise more palatable, while at the same time not making it so enticing that suicide became a desirable option. This is where end-of-life suffering fits in. Remember, suffering itself is not evil; rather, it is our ability to sense when evil is threatening us.[58] And

[58] John Paul II, *Salvifici Dolores*, 7.

evil is not an entity that is in opposition to God but is instead the absence of goodness, just like dark is the absence of light.[59] Suffering, then, is our ability to sense that we are lacking some required good. For instance, hunger is our ability to sense that we need food. In the same way, end-of-life suffering is our ability to sense when our bodies are breaking down and that death is approaching. This warning system is useful in a variety of ways. First of all, because the process is highly uncomfortable, it makes us understand that living an extended corporal life is both untenable and undesirable. By systematically (in most cases) making the daily routines that we enjoy more and more difficult, end-of-life suffering gradually opens us up to the reality that there is a better place. Eventually, daily life becomes so painful and difficult to navigate that we become ready to die, and our loved ones, seeing us struggle so mightily, become ready to let us go. In fact, they will see the end of our earthly suffering as a gift of God's mercy and, although saddened by the loss, they will be more able to accept it.

Of course, if loved ones sense that the suffering we go through at the end of life is caused by God, they may become angry with Him. This anger is misplaced, however, because they fail to understand that there is no malice in God, only love, and that suffering is not meant to destroy us but to perfect us. As I discussed in chapter 5, suffering accomplishes this perfecting role through four tasks that teach us how to love unconditionally, systematically bringing us from sin to salvation if we heed its messages.

Together with suffering, death brings out love in humanity that otherwise would be lacking. As discussed above, without death, procreation would need to stop at a point in history when the human population reached the highest level it could sustain with

[59] *ST* I, q. 48, art.1.

its technologies. This would put an end to the need for separate sexes and for spousal love, which is the model God uses to explain His love for us when He calls the Church His Bride. This motif existed from the days of the Babylonian Exile, when the prophets routinely compared the unfaithful Israelites to adulteresses and harlots.[60] Without spousal love and the love between parents and children, the world would be without its most ubiquitous examples of love and self-giving.

Despite the fact that death is required for providence, we each still have the same questions about our individual situations. We want to know why, how, and when we will die, and then we want to know what happens next.

Amy Plantinga Pauw writes that "death is a frightening prospect because it destroys any illusion that we are in full control of our lives, and we are our own makers and keepers."[61] But it is more than that. Death provides real stressors at levels far beyond what we are used to. It is a life-changing event that shares commonality with other events we know. It can be compared to graduating from school in that you are finished with one aspect of your life and are moving on to something totally new. Remember the excitement of seeing what comes next, coupled with the sense of loss of what was left behind? If you had an enjoyable time in school, you might be a little less excited to be moving on than those who suffered in school and see the next step as a relief. You might also be frightened of moving on to the next step if you did not properly prepare for

---

[60] Old Testament readings relating the unfaithful Israelites to harlots or unfaithful spouses include Jer. 3:1–10; Hos. 1:1–9; Ezek. 23:1–49; Mic. 1:1–7.

[61] Amy Plantinga Pauw, "Dying Well," in *Living Well and Dying Faithfully: Christian Practices for End-of-Life Care*, ed. John Swinton and Richard Payne (Grand Rapids, MI: Eerdmans, 2009), 259.

it, doing poorly on your studies and putting so little focus on the next step that you have no commitments or plans for it. On the other hand, those who excelled in school and prearranged their next step to be what they want have no fear at all. They are, in fact, anxious to get started on their next adventure. These are the same emotions that death brings. Of course, death naturally increases these feelings because in death the stakes are much higher and the options more restricted. After all, there is absolutely no going back or taking mementos with you. The bigger factor, though, is that there will be a judgment with eternal consequences so intensely different—eternal joy versus never-ending anguish—that of course it gives everyone some anxiety.

The Prodigal Son certainly felt this kind of anxiety as he approached his father's house, reminding himself to be humble and to beg his father's forgiveness, no doubt rehearsing the words in his mind. Remember, if you can, the stress you felt waiting for the biggest result of your life, and then multiply that stress level at least ten times to think about what it could be like waiting for the final judgment. Now think about how the father diffused that anxiety in the parable of the Prodigal Son, running up to his son and hugging him, immediately and unambiguously showing the young man his complete and undeserved mercy even after his son lost half his estate with a wasteful lifestyle. He is so happy to have his son back that he holds a banquet in his son's honor. Jesus told that parable for a reason. If we return to Him, we can expect the Father to treat us just like the prodigal sons (and daughters) we are. After all, Jesus said that there is more joy in Heaven over one repentant sinner than over ninety-nine righteous people who have no need to repent (Luke 15:7).

The thing that stands out in this is that if you have adequately prepared for life after death, just like preparing for life after graduation, then you will get what you planned for and there will be far more excitement and significantly lower stress. We are told to prepare for the future from our earliest days: putting pennies in a piggy bank to save for college, learning crafts at the hands of master craftsmen, training for sports with the hopes of someday playing as a professional. It is a shame that the same energy is not put forward by most people on planning for their death, an event that is inevitable and can come at any time.

There are, of course, many reasons for this. First, most people are afraid to die, and they therefore would like to forget about how fragile life really is because dwelling on it prematurely causes unwarranted stress, which is not healthy. Second, for most people, death is not imminent, so they worry about what is right in front of them, putting longer-term considerations on the back burner. Third, many people do not understand death, so they are ill-prepared to plan for it. This may be why you are reading this book.

For the Catholic Christian, "the obedience of Jesus has transformed the curse of death into a blessing" (CCC 1009). The theology goes further, saying, "In death, God calls man to himself" (CCC 1011). This is a message consistent with that of the parable of the Prodigal Son and consistent with the purpose of suffering proposed in the last chapter. We now see how God uses punishment to rehabilitate rather than destroy, since the objective of suffering and death, the punishments for Original Sin, is to bring about the salvation of man in the presence of God. Seen in this context, suffering and death are also signs of His mercy and forgiveness as He waits with open arms if we choose to return home.

Because of Christ, Christian death has a positive meaning since, if we die with Christ, we will also live with Him. The Church teaches that we died with Christ sacramentally when we were baptized into a new life as part of His Body, the Church. If we die in

Christ's grace, then that physical death completes the dying with Christ and so completes our incorporation in His redeeming act and assures us of living with Him forever. Note, however, that if we still have insufficient love in our hearts to avoid sin, that weakness will be corrected in Purgatory prior to entry into Heaven (CCC 1010). If, on the other hand, you loved God, because He is the essence of all that is good and true, and you responded to His call to share in the divine nature by living according to the Beatitudes, and you were content in what you had in life and wanted the best for those around you, then a very different experience awaits you on the other side of death, which is the gateway that leads to the Kingdom of God and eternal life.

Those who do not believe in God or an afterlife stare at death, seeing not the gate to eternal life but only a grave. For this reason, some facing death will turn to medicine to try to extend their earthly lives. When they do this, they neglect two realities. The first is that medicine is limited to healing the material body while man is a composite creature, with both a material body and a spiritual soul. Theological death occurs when the soul leaves the body. Medicine cannot heal the spiritual soul and God remains the master of life and death, so it is irrational to believe that medicine can stave off death. The second reality is that even if the person were fabulously successful and could indeed live forever on earth, there is not enough in the physical world to keep him interested for eternity. Consider this: If you had in abundance every material thing you wished for, living with other people of the same mindset, would you be happy? How long? For a while, you might think you are in Heaven. But all the material goods in the universe lose their appeal over time, and then you would come to the crushing realization that what makes these possessions worthwhile is their rarity and the ability to share them with others you love, things you took for granted. This is the torture endured by spoiled people who can get whatever they want, and it helps explain why so many who "have it all" find it necessary to resort to drugs or alcohol to mask their unhappiness.

This highlights the importance of suffering in God's plan. People who want to live forever in these human bodies have not yet benefited from terminal suffering. As our bodies break down, it becomes more and more obvious that we were not meant to live this way forever. At some point, the suffering becomes so unbearable that the grave seems more appealing than continuing the life we are living. In fact, having lost hope and realizing that he is not in control over his own destiny, the despondent self-centered person may seek to temporarily regain that control by ending his own life. This can be accomplished with the help of a physician through the administration of deadly drugs, which is becoming legal in more and more localities. It can also be done through terminal sedation, where the patient is heavily sedated and then denied artificial hydration and nutrition, resulting in death in about a week.

Taking death into one's own hands could easily end up backfiring on a person who, seeking to escape transitory earthly suffering, separates himself from God and finds himself suffering for eternity in Hell. While it is true the Church recognizes there can be extenuating circumstances that can diminish the responsibility of the one committing suicide, and that God in His mercy can provide the opportunity for salutary repentance, it is also true that suicide is contrary to love of God, neighbor, and ourselves (CCC 2280–2283).

Chapter 8

Particular Judgment, Heaven, Hell, and Purgatory

Following death, we are told, there is a particular judgment (CCC 1022). Completed at the moment of each person's death, this judgment first determines if one is in the state of grace. This is the check about whether you love God and want to share in His life, and it is validated by the lack of unreconciled mortal sin on one's soul. Clearly, you cannot truly love God if you publicly and purposely oppose His will and do not bother to try to reconcile when He has made reconciliation so easy to accomplish. To die in mortal sin without repenting and accepting God's merciful love means remaining separated from Him forever by our own free choice. This state of definitive self-exclusion from communion with God and the blessed is called Hell (CCC 1033).

Imagine you know Heaven exists but you are denied access. That is Hell. That is how the Church Fathers understand Hell, as absence from God, which is so painful that traditionally it has been depicted as wallowing in a burning cesspool in which the reprobate is further tortured by demons (CCC 1034-1035). This is just to show that Hell is as bad as it gets, because it is beyond our imaginations and ability to describe what a place devoid of God's love and protection would be like.

Why would a loving God create Hell? Because He respects human autonomy and desires our companionship, He does not force us to join Him in Heaven. Heaven is open to anyone who desires to be with God and shows that desire by ending life in His graces. This is not a high bar and can be achieved in minutes because our merciful and loving God wants nothing more than to be united with His children, no matter what we have done in life. To enter the state of grace, a person needs to become a member of the Body of Christ, His Church, which is done through Baptism (CCC 1262-1267).

If we should fail to live according to the dictates of the Church and our baptismal promises, we will fall from grace through mortal sin. Mortal sin is not trivial—it must be of grave matter and done with full knowledge and complete consent (CCC 1259-1261). It is not a mistake or an accident, but the person consciously and deliberately acting actively against God, knowing that doing so means separation from God and potential damnation to Hell. No one who truly loves God would do this.

What if a person later realizes that separating himself from God through sin was a bad choice? No matter how bad the sin is, God still wants us back. In His mercy, God gave the Church Confession, a sacrament of reconciliation by which a sinner can be forgiven and returned to grace if she contritely confesses her sins to a priest and carries out a penance that the priest, acting as Christ, deems appropriate (CCC 1468-1470).

What if a person truly never had knowledge of the necessity of Baptism or did not have access to the sacrament? Consistent with a loving God who wants us to join Him in the afterlife, the Church presumes that those people who would have desired Baptism had they known about it and lived a righteous life to prove it, would be somehow given the chance to choose to live in God's Kingdom as they are dying (CCC 1260).

It is obvious the particular judgment has a second stage that assesses our love and allows us to pass to Heaven. Jesus is the judge, and He gave us the criteria in the parable of the Last Judgment (Matt. 25:31-46). Those who loved their suffering neighbors would "inherit the kingdom prepared for you from the foundation of the world" (Matt. 25:34). Those who failed to minister to the needs of their suffering neighbors were told, "Depart from me, you accursed, into the eternal fire prepared for the devil and his angels" (Matt. 25:41).

It is likely that very few people share in the divine nature in their lifetimes, able to live according to the Beatitudes as Jesus did, being willing to suffer for the benefit of others. Fortunately for most of us, God does not demand this level of holiness be achieved in this life on earth. Because He is merciful and wants us to return to Him willingly, God has lowered the bar to salvation: we must simply die in the state of grace. "All who die in God's grace and friendship, but still imperfectly purified, are indeed assured of their eternal salvation; but after death they undergo purification, so as to achieve the holiness necessary to enter the joy of heaven" (CCC 1030).

The Church calls this final purification Purgatory. She formulated her doctrine on Purgatory especially at the Councils of Florence and Trent based on references by Jesus to a purifying fire before the final judgment and references in the Book of Maccabees that atonement could be made for the dead (CCC 1031-1032). Since the damned in Hell cannot be helped and the blessed in Heaven do not need help, there is a logical necessity for Purgatory to exist as some kind of holding area, adjacent to Heaven and opening up to it, for those that die in the state of grace to be purified. Although we do not know the exact process, we can hypothesize that the requirement is analogous to the four tasks of suffering that teach us to love ourselves, God, and our neighbors, leading ultimately to self-sacrificing love; thus, suffering would continue its work of identifying our needs in Purgatory.

Purgatory is a beautiful concept because it makes Heaven infinitely more accessible for fallen man and is consistent with a loving God, whose greatest desire is to reunite with His prodigal children. It is likely that few people ever reach the level of self-sacrificial love in their earthly life that is necessary to keep one from ever sinning, a requirement for direct entry into heaven; but with Purgatory, as long as we end life in the state of grace, we know we will spend eternity in Heaven once we have been cleansed. This knowledge, if fully embraced, will make earthly suffering easier to bear because we know that if we heed the message and learn to love, we reduce the effort we will need in Purgatory. When we get to Purgatory, we should be overjoyed because we know that it is just a matter of time (possibly shortened by the prayers and supplications of the living and the saints in Heaven) before we enter Heaven.

Of necessity, the experience of Hell is far different from that of Purgatory because of its inhabitants, who must actively oppose God until they die, even as they deny His existence. The kind of person that choses Hell over Heaven is one who hates rather than loves, one who seeks to exploit rather than help his weak neighbors. For these people, the absence of God seems to be a convenience, just as the lack of some good force to stop them was desired in their earthly life. They also tend to be arrogant and foolish at the same time, each one thinking they know what is best for themselves and confident that they can control their neighbors. Imagine existing in an environment where every creature is out to exploit everyone else, where no one is interested in helping anyone else except for selfish reasons. Because God actively tries to save every soul, no one ends up in Hell by accident but by their choice.

And then there are those who experience Heaven, who will be able to see the Creator face-to-face. To see God is to see all that is true and good in the universe. Called the Beatific Vision, this sight fills every human need, resulting in inexpressible happiness. This is far beyond what any living being has experienced, so words do not exist to adequately represent what this will be like. Scripture describes the Beatific Vision with happy images: paradise, wedding feasts, light, peace, the father's house, the heavenly Jerusalem (CCC 1027).

To put this in perspective, consider the internet, which is man's best attempt to assemble all the knowledge it has collectively gathered in the unconscious desire to know God. Despite being contaminated with all kinds of lies and filth, and plagued with connectivity and bandwidth issues, it still has the power to enthrall. Imagine having unlimited bandwidth and connectivity to the imagination of the Creator of all things through your mind. That is Heaven. There you will see God face to face, immersed in the Beatific Vision, which is to experience all that is good and true in the universe, to experience the full imagination of the infinite God, from which you will never grow bored (CCC 1023). And you will share this with the Trinity, the Virgin Mary, all the angels and all the people who loved as you loved. "Heaven is the ultimate end and fulfillment of the deepest human longings, the state of supreme, definitive happiness" (CCC 1024).

Do people really choose hell over heaven? Yes, every time we chose to do something self-centered rather than for the common good, we are making that choice. Any time we deny the existence of God or the value of His Church or prefer the darkness to the light, we are making that choice. Every time we choose the material gifts over the eternal spiritual ones, we make that choice. Whenever we choose our own counsel or that of unholy people over that offered by the Church and those that love us, we make that choice. Finally, every time we fail to treat others as we would want to be treated, we make that choice.

Chapter 9

The Last Day

The Church teaches that this universe will end on the final day of history. On that day, Jesus will come in His glory to judge the living and the dead. There will be the resurrection of the dead of both the just and the unjust and they will be gathered before Christ, along with the living on the last day. Jesus will separate them one from another as a shepherd separates the sheep from the goats (CCC 1038). In the presence of Christ, the truth of each person's relationship to God will be laid bare, with the consequences of the persons actions or inactions shown to them (CCC 1039). The unjust will be sent away to eternal punishment while the righteous into eternal life (CCC 1038).

At the end of time, the Kingdom of God will come in its fullness. After the universal judgment, the righteous will reign forever with Christ, glorified in body and soul. At this time, the universe will be renewed, along with humanity, perfectly re-established in Christ (CCC 1042). We are told that the new heavens and the new earth will feature the heavenly Jerusalem, where God will dwell among the community of the redeemed. "The beatific vision, in which God opens himself in an inexhaustible way to the elect, will be the ever-flowing wellspring of happiness, peace and mutual communion" (CCC 1045). The *Catechism*, quoting St. Irenaeus, shares that the visible universe is to be transformed "so that the world, restored to its original state, facing no further obstacles, should be at service to the just," sharing the glorification of the living Christ (CCC 1047).

So why does God need to redo everything and what will make it different from the present age? Two things stand out. The first is God's actual presence in the new Earth whereas he never resides in Eden or the old Earth. The second is that everyone who is admitted has freely chosen to come and has demonstrated the ability to love completely and unconditionally either during their lives on Earth or in Purgatory. It thus appears that the present earth exists to enable us to decide whether we want to be part of this new Kingdom that requires us to love others enough to put their needs above our own. We demonstrate our true desires, not with words, but with actions when we do that consistently in life.

The teaching on the last day brings everything into focus and helps us understand God's plan. We now understand the endgame, so all the other intermediate parts start to make sense. First, we now understand why everything in this world is transitory, including our lives. The world was not built to last because it is going to be replaced.

The scenario of life being an opportunity for us to assess entry into the heavenly kingdom explains the existence of evil and suffering. Evil is necessary for us to see and experience what life is like without God. Suffering makes it uncomfortable when we lack a required good and drives us to resolve the problem by obtaining the good. Suffering gives off different feelings to help us discern what the problem is. For instance, if we are hungry, we know we need food; if we are lonely, we need companionship.

Sometimes God puts evil in our lives so that we can experience the alternative to life with Him, and sometimes it is to make it clear to us that this is not our permanent home. This can be why we experience loss of material goods to physical evils. It shows us the transitory nature of material goods and that relying on them is a fool's errand. This explains why Christ and His Church preach that we should be seeking treasure in Heaven rather that treasure on earth, which will be lost. Jesus concludes that "where your treasure is, there also will your heart be" (Matt. 6:19-21).

The biggest question has always been what God wants from humanity. With the parable of the Prodigal Son, Jesus told us the answer to the question in very clear terms that no one could miss: He wants us to be with Him. The story has a dynamic that we can all grasp. In the parable, the father shows the depths of his love, mercy, and forgiveness by running to his son with open arms, not even mentioning that the son had wasted his share of the estate (Luke 15:11-32).

As magnanimous as the father's actions were in that story, though, they pale in comparison to what God has actually done and plans to do. In the parable, the father forgave the son who lost his property. In real life, God forgave the sinners that killed His Son. In doing this, God has demonstrated that His love and forgiveness know no bounds. We now see that the Christians of the first centuries were not exaggerating when they claimed that the world was created for the sake of the Church (CCC 760). They understood that God created the world for the sake of human- ity, in order to share Himself with us in love, and that He was establishing a Kingdom in which those who were willing to share their lives with Him would reside in perfect happiness. It now becomes clear that the main reason the world exists is to populate the Kingdom of God with people who want to be there with God and who have learned to love divinely. This is why Jesus told the Sadducees there was no marriage in Heaven (Matt. 22:30). If there was marriage and procreation in Heaven, then the people born in Heaven would not have had the opportunity to learn to love through suffering and to decide that self-giving love is what drives our ultimate happiness. It is through suffering that we learn the value and nature of the good, and it is the thought that sin begets evil, destroying the good that comes from our union with God, that compels us not to sin.

We also come to understand the necessity of the Church for mankind. First of all, Christ founded and sustains His holy Church, the community of believers, as a visible organization through which He communicates truth and grace to all people (CCC 771). We see the truth about the Catholic Church: it is truly God's Kingdom on earth, a community of people pledged to live the Christian life, which literally means living as Jesus did as best we can. We need to approach this as both the Body and the Bride of Christ.

As the Body of Christ, we are called to fulfill His mission, to love as He would love. And to help us discern what this means, God has given us the gift of suffering. If we alleviate suffering, we are doing God's will and loving as He would love. If we are causing suffering, we are separating ourselves from God and His Body, the Church. Admittedly, the Church is a hospital for sinners, and not all members will live according to Christian principles. This is true, sadly, even of some of the clergy. But the Church, like any other organization of humans, should not be judged based on her wayward members but on the saints, those who have demonstrated the ability to live the Christian life to its fullest extent.

As the Bride of Christ, we need to work to keep the marriage whole using our knowledge of what human marriage requires. We need to be faithful, putting God first, and we need to care for His children, our neighbors, in the ways and with the skills He has given us. We need to share in the life of the Church, participating in her liturgies and ministries, just as we need to share in the life of our spouses. At the same time, we need to make Jesus and His Church a central part of our lives, just as we do with our spouses. If we do this, we can partake of the divine nature, living as Jesus did. This act of living as both the Bride and the Body of Christ prepares us to enter into His Kingdom. At the same time, so do suffering and death, although neither will exist in God's Kingdom, as their roles are no longer necessary in a place where everyone loves profoundly, everyone has been given a new incorruptible body, and our needs are met by God Himself. As we have seen with the four tasks, suffering provides both the impetus and the opportunity to love on earth and thus prepares us to love unconditionally and fully in the new Kingdom. If suffering teaches us what we need to know and do in the new Kingdom, then dying is the final preparation, which no one can avoid, and death is the entry to the Kingdom.

God manages the timing of our deaths as a part of His plan. We should assume there are several factors in consideration. One is our readiness to enter Heaven. The book of Wisdom states that some people die young, after pleasing the Lord by their lives, to save them from future temptation (Wisd. 4:7–14). It stands to reason that a loving God may extend some people's lives until they find Him. It also makes sense that our interaction with others plays a role in the timing of our deaths. God may keep us on earth longer if He wants us to positively influence others by how we live our lives, or He may give us a short life if we are negative influences on others and He sees that will not change. At the same time, there may be situations where our deaths are impactful for His plan. Some people die inspiring deaths that save souls, others die atrocious deaths that serve as a warning for others. For example, children with fatal disabilities live short lives because their mission in life is to teach their parents to love unconditionally, and after they have completed their mission, God calls them home, ending their suffering.

The teaching on the last four things is critical to understanding suffering and death because it provides meaning and purpose to our lives, which in turn gives meaning to why we suffer and die. To make it explicit, our time on earth was granted to us by a loving and merciful God so that we can freely decide whether we love God and want to be part of His Kingdom. He left the universe unfinished and imperfect and made us the stewards of it to give us challenges and a sense of purpose to foster our growth. He gave us suffering to detect the evil in the world and made it uncomfortable so that we would shun evil and obtain the good we lack.

At the optimum time, after centuries of prophecies to announce it, He sent His only-begotten Son, Jesus Christ, in human form to preach about the Kingdom, inviting all to join via the Church that He established on earth and left in the hands of St. Peter and his successors to explain the choices before us and how we needed to "sign up." In His great mercy, God makes it easy to sign up for His Kingdom—we need only to be baptized, and He will even work with us if that is a problem.

From that point on, we must demonstrate the depth of our love for Him, ourselves, and our neighbors by doing for them what we would want them to do for us. Doing this will keep us from mortal sin, which would require a significant affront to the Lord. If we do fall from grace through sin, we need to reconcile with God sacramentally. This is not a huge imposition to apologize to God for our opposition to His will, particularly if we come to realize that God always has our best interests in mind and that resisting Him is resisting what is best for us.

In His mercy and out of love, God gave us suffering to protect us and direct us on our way home to Him by detecting any evil that threatens us. Death is the doorway to God's Kingdom, where our Creator waits for us with open arms. Death has no sting for the faithful Christian and is not to be feared. Death is also the end of our test on earth. This is, in itself, a sign of God's mercy and love because He lets us test the alternatives to decide whether we want to enter His Kingdom. He has invited us all to partake of it. If we have decided to say yes to His invitation by getting baptized and stay faithful by fulfilling our baptismal promises, then we wait in joyful anticipation for God to call us home with death. We should not be surprised if He celebrates our arrival like the father of the Prodigal Son in Jesus' parable, for Jesus told us this story to explain how the Father loves each of us and His words seem to take on a new meaning in this context: "Let us celebrate with a feast, because this son of mine was dead, and has come to life again; he was lost, and has been found" (Luke 15:23-24).

Section II

Dying with Grace

Chapter 10

What Kills Us

To die requires one of our key physiological systems to shut down. This can only happen in a finite number of ways, and each has implications for the dying person. Some deaths are quick and unexpected, which minimizes the suffering but also does not allow time for preparing your soul or your survivors for life after your death. Other deaths are long and drawn out, which means that we have elongated suffering but also time to reconcile with God and provide for our survivors.

Injuries

First, a critical organ can be damaged to the extent that it no longer functions. Injuries can be inflicted in many ways, some a complete surprise and others predictable because we recognize the situation to be dangerous. Everyone is susceptible to death by injury, although some people, such as soldiers, firefighters, and those in police forces, face more danger than others. Yet in the highest-income economies, only 6 percent of deaths are due to injuries, half of them self-inflicted when including drug and alcohol abuse.[62] By comparison, the number of deaths resulting from injury are roughly double in the lowest income economies. The differences reflect the presence in more wealthy communities of both enhanced safety precautions to prevent injuries and better care to keep injuries from becoming fatal.

With the exception of deaths that are self-induced or those resulting from capital punishment, deaths from serious injuries are unexpected, and most lead to a quick demise. The three most prevalent causes in all economic environments are traffic fatalities, drowning, and falls.[63] In many cases, the dying will not realize they are in danger until death is upon them. One can imagine that in many of these situations, the individual may be dead before even realizing what happened. There may not be any pain, but whatever there is, is certainly short-lived in most cases.

Unfortunately, unexpected injuries find most individuals unprepared for their death. Unless they are highly organized and devout, people may find themselves unprepared to meet God, having died with unreconciled mortal sins on their souls. For those that are devout and keep themselves in the state of grace, a relatively quick, painless death is a great blessing, but it is a curse for the person who has not taken the effort to reconcile with God.

Our survivors suffer intensely from our unexpected deaths because our absence will leave a void for them in every aspect of life that we previously filled. If we have been diligent in preparing

---

[62] "Global Health Estimates 2019: Estimated Deaths by Cause and Region, 2000 and 2019," World Health Organization, https://cdn.who.int/media/docs/default-source/gho-documents/global-health-estimates/ghe2019_cod_wbincome_2000_201933383745-a750-4d94-8491-fb209dcece6f_7c1ac8d4-d425-4deb-8a12-1dc26c293e80.xlsx?sfvrsn=e7bafa8_9.

[63] Ibid.

for death, as I will discuss in chapter 13, we can mitigate the pain of this void to some extent. While these actions will help ease the burden on the survivors, they will not answer the questions about why the person died this way and at this time. Because many injuries appear to be preventable, and at the same time random, some survivors blame themselves or the deceased for the death for not being more careful, while others blame God. This can be useful in that it calls to attention dangerous situations for others to avoid, but only if it is publicized so they know of the danger.

Survivors should take heart in the knowledge that nothing is random with an all-seeing, all-powerful God who loves us and thus arranges our deaths in a way to save the most souls, including our own. Keeping this in mind, we may be able to discern the reasons for a loved one's death. In some cases, our loved ones may have been sacrificed to call attention to unsafe conditions or situations that will save others in the future. For the devout who die of injuries, the point might be to demonstrate to others how to die faithfully. If that does not seem fair, we should recognize that if the deceased understood this fact and willingly accepted it as part of God's plan, it is redemptive.

Nutritional Deficiency

The second way that death can occur is if the organs are denied the raw materials and the living conditions required to sustain life. In high-income economies, there are enough government programs and independent charities to make death from nutritional deficiencies almost negligible (0.3 percent). In low-income countries, the chances of dying from malnutrition are 1.4 percent, down by a factor of 2 over the last twenty years.[64] These deaths

---

[64] Ibid.

identify a lack of charity on the part of their neighbors and hopefully will motivate those who failed to help to change their ways and provide for the future poor. Those who suffer in this way can offer up their suffering to Jesus for the good of the souls of all the people that witness their poverty, not only for individuals who respond with charity but also for those who do not, in order to soften their hearts.

Infectious Diseases

Third, our immune system can fail to provide protection against infectious diseases (bacteria, viruses). For centuries, this was the scourge of civilization, with plagues devastating the world. However, medical science has made such inroads in immunology that even in the COVID-19 pandemic, the high-income economies had only 2 percent of deaths attributed to infectious and parasitic diseases in 2019.[65] The rate was roughly twelve times higher (23.9 percent) in low-income countries that cannot afford vaccines and other immune-system boosting drugs, but that level is down significantly from the 38.9 percent that existed in the low-income countries in the year 2000, the result of increased charity on the part of wealthier nations. Those who die of infectious diseases tend to be the weakest individuals in society: the very young, whose immune systems are not fully developed, or those whose immune systems have been compromised by other diseases (particularly the elderly).

Infectious diseases are actually battles to the death between our immune systems and microscopic invaders. If our immune systems are fully functional, then the chances of expelling most viruses are extremely good. Typically, but not always, the illness is short,

[65] Ibid.

with either the virus being expelled or the patient dying within a number of days. In a recent study of hospitalized COVID-19 patients, the median time from first symptom to death was only 18.5 days, and those who survived were released from the hospital in twenty-two days.[66] The chance of surviving the hospital stay was 72 percent, but only 22 percent of the cases progressed to the ICU. For comparison, the Black Death that decimated Europe, killing 30–60 percent of its population from 1347–1351, usually killed within three days.[67]

Some infectious diseases, however, can cause a lingering death if not treated with modern drugs. My paternal grandmother, Leona Gastonguay Chaloux, for example, suffered for seven years in a sanatorium with tuberculosis before succumbing on June 15, 1945. If she had caught the disease today, she would be treated with one of four medicines for six months and most likely be completely cured.[68]

If you have an infectious disease serious enough to go to the hospital, then you should ask for last rites (Confession, Anointing of the Sick, Viaticum) if you are Catholic, reconciling yourself to God and His Church while you still have time (CCC 1525).

[66] "How do COVID-19 Symptoms Progress and What Causes Death?" Medical Answers, Drugs.com, March 28, 2022, https://www. drugs.com/medical-answers/covid-19-symptoms-progress-death -3536264/.

[67] Lizzie Wade, "From Black Death to Fatal Flu, Past Pandemics Show Why People on the Margins Suffer Most: Inequality Made Historical Pandemics 'Worse Than They Had to Be,'" *Science*, May 14, 2020, https://www.science.org/content/article/black-death-fatal -flu-past-pandemics-show-why-people-margins-suffer-most.

[68] "Questions and Answers about Tuberculosis," Centers for Disease Control and Prevention, accessed July 12, 2022, https://www.cdc. gov/tb/publications/faqs/tb-qa.htm#why-tb-prob.

If you are not currently Catholic, this might be your last chance for Baptism. Even this limited time to accomplish reconciliation with God is a blessing those with serious infections receive if they are disposed to take advantage of it. For some people, the realization that they are on their deathbed is the impetus they need to turn to God. And those who are already devout may contract an infectious disease to spur other less devout sufferers to turn to God by the manner in which they suffer, making it redemptive for them as well.

Because we are in mortal combat with our microscopic invaders, most of our energy should and will be used to fight that fight until either the invaders are killed or we are, leaving little time or energy for passing on our affairs to others. This is why it is so important to plan for death in an ongoing fashion.

Bodily Breakdown

Finally, for those of us who survive or avoid life-threatening injuries, nutritional deficiencies, and infectious diseases, our bodies break down when we have failure of major organs or cancers, which cause the organs to malfunction. Most people expect this breakdown to begin in their seventies, but if you have a genetic disease that stresses particular parts of the body, it can be as early as five years old (Tay-Sachs). In the highest income economies, fully 86 percent of deaths result from noncontagious diseases, 30 percent from cancer and 56 percent from major organ failure.[69] This means that the vast majority of people in the industrialized world will get a terminal diagnosis, experience terminal suffering, and die of a terminal disease. This is a scenario that most people think about when considering death because it is so prevalent and

[69] World Health Organization, "2019: Estimated Deaths."

also because its dynamics allow us to consider the way we are living, where and how we die, and what happens after that.

When a person is diagnosed with a terminal illness, it disrupts all the person's plans and raises questions about whether social, psychological, physical, and spiritual needs can be met. Indeed, terminal suffering often causes family members to struggle to meet a loved one's physical and social needs, requiring most people to seek professional help, whether in the form of in-home nursing care, senior assisted-living facilities, or, in the most extreme cases, nursing homes and hospitals.

This brings us to the point of how it is decided where we will live out the rest of our lives. We should be able to stay in our own homes as long as we can safely live independently, and no one should press us to do otherwise. Provided we are sound of mind and free of dementia, we should make the decisions that affect where and how we live. If we do not feel safe being left alone, then we should either hire an in-home aide or move to an assisted-living community out of fairness and charity for our loved ones, who need to live their own lives and cannot devote themselves to twenty-four-hour care indefinitely. Everyone needs time off.

Generally, people start off thinking they will be happiest living in the comfort of their own home, but it is not always the case. Many of today's assisted-living communities offer activities and social opportunities that provide solutions to the loneliness and boredom that many seniors have when living alone. And some individuals will feel safer in an environment that has trained medical professionals monitoring their health.

Once dementia sets in and you become fully dependent on others for daily living activities, then you need professional care, and it will no longer be your decision. This is an excruciating decision for your caregivers, which they will not take lightly. It is not that they do not have time for you or that they love you less if they seek professional care. In fact, it is probably the best for everyone involved, and it does not mean they will not visit. It is an act of love to accept the situation.

When my paternal grandfather, Andre Chaloux, a man who persevered through tremendous suffering in his life, developed dementia, his declining health led to two decisions made entirely out of love. The first was to sell his businesses, which he could no longer maintain, and move into a small residential home that my grandmother could maintain on her own after he died. The second was for my grandmother, Marguerite Rancourt Chaloux, to commit him to a nursing home when his dementia made him confused and violent. This was not abandoning him, because for the remaining two years of his life, she visited him in the home daily from opening to close, taking care of him even though he no longer recognized her. It was an amazing show of love, especially considering that my grandmother, who never learned to drive, commuted by whatever means were available to her, getting rides with her stepchildren or grandchildren, taking a taxi, or, at times, walking the half mile to the home.

My grandmother lived two more years in the comfortable home my grandfather had left her. I visited one weekend a month, staying with her when I came to visit my maternal grandfather, Joe Murdock. She began to complain about back pain, so my uncle Marcel took her to the doctor. We were all shocked to hear she had terminal skin cancer and had been given six months to live. I drove up to Maine that weekend only to find out she died in her home during my five-hour trip. Recognizing her as one of the most loving and selfless people we have ever met, my family was confident God called her home so quickly because she was prepared to enter His Kingdom and did not need to suffer any longer. What we learn from this is that doctors cannot be expected to accurately predict time of death and that not every incidence of cancer or organ breakdown provides the time to close out our affairs, so it is important to be proactive.

To die well is to be able to reconcile with God and our neighbors, to feel that we have completed our life's work, and to train those who follow to do the same. But the only thing that really matters is whether you join with God in the Beatific Vision. This is possible for all people who are so diligent in following Church teaching that they are ready for death at any time. However, there is a special grace given to those who have a terminal diagnosis, because God has given us advance warning to take the necessary steps to enter His Kingdom and to set up our survivors to do the same. Rejoice in His love for you, especially if you are not yet prepared to die, since He has granted you that preparation time. But do not be complacent about it—instead, address your preparation with urgency, since as my grandmother's case shows, our deaths cannot be accurately predicted.

Going through the dying process—being diagnosed as terminally ill or injured and then experiencing terminal suffering—seems harsh, but it actually possesses some significant benefits in addition to making it potentially easier to be in the state of grace. We have the opportunity when we die to be in a safe, comfortable environment, surrounded by loved ones, content with having accomplished our life goals. We have an opportunity to reach closure on our earthly affairs diligently and well with our survivors and to pass on whatever they need to carry on without us. And remember, taking the time to bring any earthly activities to closure and to provide for the people who have been dependent on us is a form of loving our neighbors. This of course includes settling all debts and grievances, particularly those with family members. Another important benefit of the dying process is that we can transfer what we have learned to our survivors, especially our experiences with suffering and death, so our loved ones can overcome their fear of these experiences by understanding that God loves us. Finally, because the suffering is harsh and is apparent to the survivors, it makes the process of letting go much easier and the transition to the next life more desirable.

Does this mean that all terminally ill patients die well? Not at all. It depends on how they receive the information and what they do with it. First of all, not everyone with a terminal illness knows the severity of their situation. A terminal diagnosis is as hard to deliver as it is to receive, and as I noted previously, many physicians believe death is a failure of medicine, so they may withhold the true diagnosis or even deny it, choosing instead to sugarcoat it, saying that there are potential cures in development. And, of course, sometimes there are. After all, the American Cancer Society tells us there are 16.9 million cancer survivors in the United States alone.[70] But if a doctor really believes a case is terminal—meaning that there is no cure and it will be fatal—he does a great service to the patient by letting the patient know. Bad news is better than uncertainty because at least you can plan with bad news. With uncertainty, all that is left for the person to do is to worry, which is another way to suffer.

---

[70] American Cancer Society, *Cancer Facts & Figures 2022* (Atlanta: American Cancer Society, 2022), 3.

Chapter 11

Choices for Treatment

For those who are dying, the Church has a special sacrament, the Anointing of the Sick, which confers a special grace on the Christian experiencing the difficulties inherent in the condition of grave illness or old age (CCC 1527). This sacrament has the following effects:

- forgiving sins, restoring a person to the state of grace
- providing the strength, peace, and courage to endure suffering
- uniting the person's suffering to Christ for his own good and that of the whole Church (similar to what one seeks when offering suffering of any kind up to God)
- the restoration of health (only if it is conducive to the salvation of the soul)
- preparing for passing over to eternal life (CCC 1532)

This sacrament meets a variety of needs that many of the dying have but does so in ways that will be good for the person's soul. In fact, it directs us to what we should be doing with our terminal suffering.

There are several important points to note about this sacrament. The very first and most profound effect of this sacrament is that by requesting it, the person has publicly declared a desire to be with Christ, offering up suffering for the good of the Church, which is redemptive. This in turn gives the suffering purpose, providing the strength, peace, and courage to endure the pain, and prepares us for passing over to eternal life. The restoration of health only proceeds from this sacrament if it is conducive to the salvation of the soul. This tells us that, often, becoming healthy is not required for the good of the soul, but at times it might be. This is not to say that we should not seek healing, only that we must discern whether to do so inhibits us from also pursuing the salvation of the soul.

The first decision a newly diagnosed terminally ill patient will have to face is how aggressively to fight the disease — or whether to fight it at all. Indeed, a doctor might give the patient four options on how to proceed with a terminal illness. These options are understandably quite diverse, reflecting different moral standards.

In the secular medical community today, terminally ill patients will be given four discreet options on how to proceed, but Catholic healthcare services will only offer the first two options:

- Fight the disease until you are cured or dead.
- Embrace your natural death.
- Sleep through the illness with terminal sedation.
- Control your death through physician-assisted suicide (PAS).

Fight It

The first option, the default choice in the United States, is to treat the disease aggressively until the patient is either cured or dead. In fact, for almost four hundred years, the medical community has been taking up that fight for humanity, dating back at least to Sir Francis Bacon, who in the seventeenth century declared a new goal for medicine to use science to heal all injuries and illnesses and, ultimately, to extend life indefinitely.[71]

The medical community has done amazing things since then, finding ways to cure most infectious diseases and replace worn-out organs, and as a result there are 16.9 million Americans who are cancer survivors.[72] This is a track record people believe in, particularly the doctors who claim "death is a failure of medicine."[73] For people who are desperate to live, it is an easy sell for a physician to say, "We have an experimental solution that has the potential to save your life," and get a positive response from the patient, who figures nothing is more valuable than maintaining life.

The truth of it is twofold: there are indeed things more valuable than your mortal life, and there are also limits to medicine. Consider the case of Lisa, a young mother with two small girls, who had breast cancer. Lisa's friend suggested that she write her life story for her kids when they got older, which she resolved to do. But Lisa and her doctor were both confident Lisa would be cured, so she put off writing it, opting instead to invest her time and energy into treatments. Two weeks later she was dead, having never written her legacy stories for her children to cherish.[74]

As heartrending as that story is, we must recognize that the overwhelming societal sentiment is that your life is your most important asset, and you should do everything in your power to

[71] Allen Verhey, *The Christian Art of Dying: Learning from Jesus* (Grand Rapids, MI: Eerdmans, 2011), 28-29.

[72] American Cancer Society, *Cancer Facts & Figures 2022* (Atlanta: American Cancer Society, 2022), 3.

[73] John Swinton, "Why Me, Lord?" in *Living Well and Dying Faithfully: Christian Practices for End-of-Life Care*, ed. John Swinton and Richard Payne (Grand Rapids, MI: Eerdmans, 2009), 127.

[74] Ibid., 112-113.

save it. In fact, as I discussed previously, the most fundamental instinct God gave mortal creatures is self-preservation. Together, the instincts to avoid suffering and death drive us to undertake the task of maintaining our physical health and well-being. This thought gets amplified with the confidence exuded by medical professionals that nothing is beyond their scope to heal. It is very easy in this environment to lose track of what is important and focus all our time and energy on fighting the disease. The problem is that when fighting this battle, we are no longer living our lives and we are not planning for the next one; so when we lose this battle, we lose not only this life but the next.

Thus, many people with a terminal diagnosis waste the opportunity it affords us to reconcile with God and put our affairs in order by ignoring everything except fighting the disease. But medicine, despite the successes, does have its limits, so turning to medical science for an answer to a terminal illness must be with the right expectations. What you can reasonably expect is control of symptoms, which allows your quality of life to be high enough to maintain your obligations to others as long as possible. It is important to keep the perspective that life has meaning and purpose and to remember that medical solutions that extend life at the cost of what gives it meaning and purpose are counterproductive. Indeed, these extensions of life serve no purpose and result in just extending the person's suffering.

In the same way, it is counterproductive to spend all our time, resources, and energy in the quest for life extension if doing so forces us to give up what imbues our lives with meaning. On the other hand, medical solutions that give us the ability to fulfill our obligations and carry out our role in God's plan are a godsend in the true meaning of the word. For instance, without the right medicine balance, I cannot type, which makes me unproductive.

It is therefore appropriate to expend energy and time to balance the medicines in a way that makes me most productive.

It is important to remember that as well as the medical community has done, it does have limits. I learned this the hard way. When I was diagnosed with hepatitis C in 2002, it was dormant in my system, causing me no discernable problem after twenty-five years. The doctor told me it was potentially fatal and that they had a cure that worked to kill the virus 90 percent of the time. I was told the drugs were strong and had vicious side effects but that I had the potential to infect my wife and children if I did not take care of it. So twenty years ago, I took on this fight—and I have been nauseous almost every day since.

Furthermore, it is pretty clear that this treatment can be directly linked to my celiac disease, which restricts my diet and, in turn, caused the gut bacteria imbalance that led to the nausea and is itself linked to Parkinson's disease. Even my GI doctor, the one who put me on the drug to begin with, told me the last time I saw him that, in retrospect, knowing what we now know, it was a fight we did not need to take on. I reminded him that we did because it protected my family from going through a similar ordeal if they came into contact with my blood. Sometimes, we need to take on suffering like this for the good of others.

If I go all the way back and trace my ongoing health problems, they are all related to a congenital heart defect, because it is almost assuredly true that I got hepatitis from the transfusions that came with the heart surgeries, and as just discussed, the hepatitis treatments can be linked to all my current health issues. There are several lessons to learn from this. First and foremost, this entire sequence, painful as it was and is, put me in the position to credibly have a ministry on suffering and death that gives me a purpose in God's plan for which I am grateful. It was obviously decades in the making, starting even before my birth, so it has nothing to do with anything I did or did not do. It is a pure gift of God.

Secondly, medicine has limits that we need to recognize, and treatments often have unexpected secondary effects, so we need to carefully assess the treatments offered to see whether the side effects are worse than the symptoms they are curing. The human body is intricate, with many overlapping processes that are finely balanced. If you change one process, it affects all the ones it interacts with, potentially causing a cascade of side effects. For instance, the medication I take to manage my Parkinson's symptoms also causes nausea, fluid retention in my limbs, and grating fatigue. The medical solution to this is to prescribe drugs to address each of these onerous side effects. These secondary drugs have their own side effects, which require additional drugs to manage—and on and on. Some doctors, in an effort to manage all the side effects, will literally prescribe multiple layers of drugs. My experience with this is that the process is exceptionally costly and does not work, because it overrides all the body's natural control systems. I prefer to minimize the drugs and apply them in a way that eases the discomfort enough that I can work through it. I do not need to feel perfect; I just need to be functional.

Third, medicine should be pursued to extend our functionality so that we can contribute more to society and, in particular, care for our families, while also caring for our souls. To the extent that treatments or medications do not help us contribute to these tasks, such treatments are counterproductive and should be avoided.

Pope Pius XII, in his November 24, 1957, address to Catholic physicians and anesthesiologists, ruled that the life-at-all-cost approach is not Christian and is not morally required. Pius stated that life is a relative and intermediate good, and because it is good, life should usually be preserved. However, the goodness of life is only possible insofar as it is directed to the greatest good.[75] In other words, one should not extend life at the expense of giving up Heaven since that is what gives it purpose and meaning. He further delineated this, saying that we are responsible for accepting ordinary care, which includes basic needs (food, water, air, and so forth) and easy-to-do medical treatments.

However, there is no obligation to accept extraordinary care—care that is repulsive to the patient, that requires great effort or cost, or that results in excessive pain or uses exotic or unproven technique.[76] Now, how do we go about assessing this? It is up to the patient to decide if the cost of treatment is disproportionate with the benefits, because every situation is different and everyone's tolerance for pain is different as well. For instance, costs that are unbearable to one family might be "pocket change" to another, or one person might think that amputating a leg to save his life is unthinkable while another is willing to sacrifice the leg to save himself.

This can be a little confusing, so let us discuss the real trade-offs. On one side is the requirement to preserve our lives as the stewards of our bodies, so we are obligated to do the basic things to preserve life, which includes providing nutrition, hydration, oxygen, and temperature control as well as easily tolerated medicines. On the other side is the concern that the cure is worse than the problem it is supposedly treating. No one is required to extend a life through

---

[75] Congregation for the Doctrine of the Faith, "Commentary," https://www.vatican.va/roman_curia/congregations/cfaith/documents/rc_con_cfaith_doc_20070801_nota-commento_en.html.

[76] USCCB Ethical And Religious Directives for Catholic Health Care Services, sixth edition, 2016, directive 57 https://www.usccb.org/resources/ethical-religious-directives-catholic-health-service-sixth-edition-2016-06_0.pdf

suffering, since suffering indicates that the cure is deficient in some way. This does not in any way justify suicide or euthanasia, because there is a huge ethical difference between killing and letting a person die. Killing is taking God's responsibility for the timing and situation of a person's death. Letting nature take its course, without turning to extraordinary intervention, is licit because it is following God's will. Note, however, the need to continue ordinary care in all cases to avoid killing the patient through neglect.

When we reach the point that we can no longer carry out our social responsibilities because of terminal suffering that the medical community cannot alleviate (in other words, when our doctors declare a terminal diagnosis), we need to switch our priority to planning for our deaths. This can be very hard for people since it will feel like we are giving up, which goes against our most basic instinct of self-preservation. We may also get pushback from loved ones, who may encourage us to try harder, to keep us around longer. Planning for our death is ultimately more productive at the end of life, but it is really hard to motivate yourself to do so without terminal suffering to drive home the point that your forthcoming death is actually going to happen. I know that the first five years I had Parkinson's I never gave my impending death a thought. And never at any time did I take it seriously with my first two terminal illness diagnoses. Only recently have I felt diminished enough to start contemplating death seriously. The result of that contemplation so far is this book.

Embrace It

The second option doctors typically offer at the end of life is hospice care. The hospice program provides an alternative approach to terminal illness, embracing natural death rather than fighting it to the bitter end. The hospice strategy is to let patients die a natural death wherever they live, whether it be in the community or in an institution. Under hospice, the dying person will receive no medical treatments except to relieve pain or other symptoms. This movement gained traction quickly after Cicely Saunders founded St. Christopher's Hospice in 1967 as the first hospice linking "expert pain and symptom control, compassionate care, teaching and clinical research."[77] In fact, the majority (52.4 percent) of Americans now die in some form of hospice care.[78] This is the choice that will resonate with people who want to die a good death with God because it allows them to prioritize living their lives and planning for death instead of searching for and undergoing new life extension treatments.

Cicely Saunders is generally credited with two legacies. The first is that the dying need more than just medical care—they need total care, including treatment for biological, psychological, social, and spiritual pain.[79] This was a much-needed transition from cure to care for those who were terminally ill, and the shift in perspective fueled the rapid growth of hospice care as people, who wanted their loved ones to die a natural, dignified death, came to understand the suffering that was being incurred in the medical establishment's futile attempt to extend life indefinitely.

The second legacy was to redefine pain as a pathology of its own, another disease to be treated. Saunders promoted the use

---

[77] "Dame Cicely Saunders Biography, Part 4," Cicely Saunders Institute, https://cicelysaundersinternational.org/dame-cicely-saunders/st-christophers-hospice.

[78] "What Percentage of Americans Receive Hospice?" 1-800-Hospice, February 18, 2020, https://www.1800hospice.com/blog/what-percentage-america.

[79] Jeffrey Bishop, *The Anticipatory Corpse* (Notre Dame, IN: The University of Notre Dame Press, 2011), 254.

of narcotics for terminally ill patients since addiction was not a concern for them.[80] This unfortunately is a misunderstanding of the role of pain in God's plan. Pain is not a disease to be cured, it is a warning that the body has sustained an injury. Pain and suffering should be alleviated by addressing the root cause. To merely deaden pain without heeding its warning is to ignore a God-sent message and should be avoided.

Granted, extreme pain can be debilitating, and end of life pain is often the most extreme. Sometimes it is necessary to mitigate the pain for a while to carry out some needed tasks. However, pain relief is counterproductive if it renders the recipient unconscious and unable to function at all.

Unfortunately, hospice has morphed over time to "palliative care," especially as the hospice program was funded by national governments and in large part absorbed by the medical community.[81] The prevailing societal view seems to be that pain is the enemy of the dying.

I have very recent experience with hospice care since my mother was in hospice until her death on Sunday, May 8, 2022. She had very severe dementia, being unable to speak or even move any part of her body other than her right hand. She was in obvious pain, so the hospice medical team's response was to keep increasing the dosage of the narcotic drug she was on. This did reduce her pain, but it also sedated her to the point that she was basically unresponsive for the last month of her life. We tried to get them to back off the dose in her last days, but they were adamant that her greatest need was to be out of pain, and they continued to treat her accordingly.

---

[80] Ibid.
[81] Bishop, *Anticipatory Corpse*, 257.

This is not only my experience with hospice. Jenny Echavarria, one of my students at the Avila Institute for Spiritual Formation, who volunteered to critique the first draft of this book, wrote me about her own experience in caring for her mother:

> I didn't want her to deal with all the pain from bile duct cancer—stage 4 when she was home and I was assigned the home hospice care. The medication prescribed I followed precisely as instructed and it put her in a catatonic state. I was informed if I didn't they would remove her from her home to the hospice center. I had promised her she would die at home. There was no way I was prepared for the experience. I'd sit in the living room and my entire body would shake as if my body was uncontrolled. I'd gather myself and go back into the room with her since I had no aide. My daughter and granddaughter were with me during the day. I felt helpless.[82]

The lesson learned here is that at the beginning of hospice care, families must establish where they stand on the consciousness-pain divide. If the patient is willing to endure some suffering in order to close out affairs, this needs to be communicated well to the hospice team when they are first engaged. If the hospice agency is affiliated with the Catholic Church, they should be aware of the need to offer pain relief without sedation because the bishops have taken the stand that patients in Catholic healthcare facilities "should be kept as free of pain as possible so that they may die comfortably and with dignity, and in the place where they wish to die. Since a person has the right to prepare for his or her death while fully conscious, he or she should not be deprived of consciousness

---

[82] Jenny Echavarria, e-mail to author, July 23, 2022.

without a compelling reason."[83] This is directive 61 of the ethical and religious directives published by the USCCB for use by the Catholic healthcare system. Show this directive to secular agencies you might engage with to gain their agreement before hiring them. If they revert to heavy sedation that you do not feel is appropriate, you can get them to stop, but you will have to be very forceful. Any indecision on your part will be taken as agreement to their expert advice. I do not think this stand comes from any malice. I believe it is due to applying compassion to different priorities. Therefore, appeal to their compassion when explaining your priorities and you should have a way to gain consensus.

Sleep through It

This brings us to the third option generally given to people dying in a secular facility, called terminal sedation. It seeks to eliminate suffering simply by heavily sedating the dying and leaving them unconscious until they die. This is almost always coupled with the removal of artificial nutrition and hydration, which obviously curtails their lives much faster, usually within a week to ten days. This practice is legal everywhere despite the objections of the Catholic Church.

Terminal sedation is typically justified by referencing the principle of double effect (PDE), albeit incorrectly. In moral theology, actions are judged based on the object of the action (what is being done) and the intent (why it is being done). For an action to be considered moral, neither the object nor the intent can be morally

---

[83] USCCB, *Ethical and Religious Directives for Catholic Health Care Services*, 6th ed. (Washington, D.C.: USCCB, 2018), no. 61, https:// www.usccb.org/about/doctrine/ethical-and-religious-directives/ upload/ethical-religious-directives-catholic-health-service-sixth-edition-2016-06.pdf.

illicit. The circumstances surrounding the action do not factor into whether the action is good or evil, but they can mitigate or increase the culpability of the person taking the action (CCC 1749–1754). To this framework, Thomas Aquinas added the insight that some actions have a secondary, unintended effect that does not affect the moral calculus because it goes beyond the intention of the actor in question and is considered just another circumstance. He famously used this to justify the accidental killing of an assailant in self-defense.[84]

Proponents of terminal sedation may invoke PDE, claiming that the intent of terminal sedation is to stop the patient from suffering, which is a moral good, and the object is the sedation of the patient, which is morally ambivalent. The fact that the patient dies is claimed to be an unintended second effect of the procedure. This is a wrong usage of the principle of double effect because the object conflates two separate actions, each of which must be evaluated on their own. The first action is the heavy sedation, which is morally illicit in that it deprives the patient of the consciousness to prepare for his or her death.[85] The second action is to withhold nutrition and hydration, the intention of which is clearly to kill the patient, an obvious moral wrong.

In the years following Vatican II, there was a lot of misuse of basic moral theology evaluation tools like this, which prompted St. John Paul II to publish *Veritatis Splendor* in 1993 to reset the foundations of moral theology and ethics so that morally illicit procedures would no longer be declared ethical. Referencing Aquinas, John Paul II makes the point that the object of the action must be "the proximate end [the first result] of a deliberate decision which

---

[84] *ST* II–II, q. 64, art. 7.
[85] USCCB, *Ethical and Religious Directives*, no. 61.

determines the act of willing on the part of the acting person."[86] To say it another way, the object is the immediate action willed by the person taking the action. John Paul II explains further, "The reason why a good intention is not itself sufficient, but a correct choice of actions is also needed, is that the human act depends on its object, whether that object is capable or not of being ordered to God, to the One who 'alone is good,' and thus brings about the perfection of the person."[87] The Church clearly teaches that suppressing the consciousness of the person indefinitely is not licit (directive 61 above), nor is it licit to deny ordinary care, so clearly this practice, which may well be the established procedure in certain hospitals, is unethical.

In 2011, my father had a massive stroke that the neurologist told us he would not recover from. They ensured that by giving him terminal sedation. This was long before I studied moral theology and ethics, so I did not understand the ethical argument presented above. I was told that they were going to sedate him to spare him the pain, and that since he had a do-not-resuscitate (DNR) order in, he would not be given food or drink and would be dead within a week. Like anyone whose father is about to die, I was not thinking as clearly as normal given the stress, but I felt queasy about this and queried the doctor about whether this was euthanasia (mercy killing). The doctor assured me that this was standard practice at the hospital and that it had been reviewed thoroughly by their ethics board—which I am sure was true, but that does not mean it is truly ethical.

---

[86] John Paul II, encyclical letter *Veritatis Splendor* (The Splendor of Truth) (August 6, 1993), no. 78 https://www.vatican.va/content/john-paul-ii/en/encyclicals/documents/hf_jp-ii_enc_06081993_veritatis-splendor.html.
[87] Ibid.

Two days later, my father attempted to get out of bed, which increased my anxiety about the situation, but the doctor assured me it was a meaningless reaction that had no thought behind it because 45 percent of my father's brain had been destroyed. Three days later, he died in the presence of five of his children, myself included, as my youngest sister read him the biography that I wrote for him. Despite the warmth of the ending, I felt and still feel that we let him down in his moment of greatest need by not knowing the Church's well-thought-out ethical viewpoint on his situation. Given what the doctor said, it is probable that withholding fluids accelerated but did not cause his death. My advice to anyone who is confronted with this problem is to continue to provide the necessities of life (ordinary care) and let God's will be done.

If you have any questions about the ethics of a procedure, ask your local parish priest, contact the National Catholic Bioethics Center,[88] or go to the USCCB's *Ethical and Religious Directives for Catholic Health Care Services*, which is available online.[89]

Control It

The fact that Catholic morality is not practiced in secular hospitals becomes more obvious in the fourth option that hospitals in many states will offer: physician-assisted suicide. Some will try to get the same feeling of a loving "death party" with loved ones sending them off by planning their own death through suicide,

---

[88] Contact the National Catholic Bioethics Center at https://www.ncbcenter.org/contact-us.

[89] USCCB's *Ethical and Religious Directives for Catholic Health Care Services*, 6th ed. (Washington, D.C.: USCCB, 2018), available online at https://www.usccb.org/about/doctrine/ethical-and-religious-directives/upload/ethical-religious-directives-catholic-health-service-sixth-edition-2016-06.pdf.

but it will not be the same. Suicide is a selfish act because it is a conscious choice to abandon those who depend on you, many of whom you may not be aware of. You cannot simply expect people to celebrate your killing yourself in the same way that they would celebrate your life if you were called home to God.

Suicide is always an immoral choice because God alone is the master of life and death, and as such, He knows the exact time and location that is optimum for each one of our deaths to bring about the salvation of souls, both ours and those around us. To take that upon ourselves is to declare that we know better than God about the timing of our death, which is ludicrous since we do not know His plan. What if He had planned for you to have a visit from someone you were estranged from years ago and you killed yourself just before that person arrived to mend your relationship? Does it not make sense to wait and see what God has in store for you? As discussed earlier, suicide is a self-centered act that fails to consider the thoughts and needs of others and is disrespectful of God, thus separating us from Him permanently, unless in His great mercy He allows you to reconcile with Him in the last moments of your life.

Recognizing God's abundant mercy, the Church leaves open this possibility, teaching that "we should not despair of the eternal salvation of persons who have taken their own lives. By ways known to him alone, God can provide the opportunity for salutary repentance. The Church prays for persons who have taken their own lives" (CCC 2283). In addition, recognizing that there can be extenuating circumstances, the Church teaches that "grave psychological disturbances, anguish, or grave fear of hardship, suffering, or torture can diminish the responsibility of the one committing suicide" (CCC 2282).

Chapter 12

Living Well with a Terminal Disease

One important thing to remember when you have been diagnosed with a terminal injury or illness is that you are not dead yet, so you still can leave a positive legacy with the time and strength you have left.

People debate over what constitutes a good life. Some believe that a good life requires comfort and pleasure. Others think of a good life in terms of wealth, power, or fame. These are all transitory goals, however, the results of which cannot be carried over after death, so they are worthless in terms of providing a good death. Love is the only currency that transcends death and can be carried over to the next world.[90] Therefore, a good life is one that seeks the love of God before all else. This is the essence of the theology presented in the first section, and it is consistent with what the *Catechism* teaches: "'All Christians in any state or walk of life are called to the fullness of Christian life and to the perfection of charity.' All are called to holiness: 'Be perfect, as your heavenly Father is perfect'" (CCC 2013).

---

[90] This is the topic of the third book in this series, *Heaven's Currency*, concerning the mystery of love.

This is an important admonition from the Church, so let us parse it out. All Christians are called to holiness, regardless of state or walk of life. First of all, this is addressed to Christians because Jesus is the way, the truth, and the life. No one comes to the Father except through Him (John 14:6). Not only did Jesus show us how this was to be done by His works and actions, but it is His grace that enables us to partake of the divine nature and become holy. Men cannot aspire to be gods without the aid of divine power and initiative. Indeed, God initiates our salvation by calling to us, and it is our free response to that invitation that has merit. We cannot earn our way to Heaven; we can only accept His invitation (CCC 2008-2011).

The Church describes it this way:

> Baptism, the door to life and to the Kingdom of God, is the first sacrament of the New Law, which Christ offered to all, that they may have eternal life. He later entrusted this sacrament and the Gospel to his Church when he told his apostles: "Go, make disciples of all nations and baptize them in the name of the Father and of the Son and of the Holy Spirit." Baptism is therefore, above all, the sacrament of that faith by which, enlightened by the grace of the Holy Spirit, we respond to the Gospel of Christ.[91]

Baptism is a covenant agreement between us and God. We become full members of the Body of Christ, and ultimately the Kingdom of God, if we follow the teachings of Christ handed down by the Church and become holy.

---

[91] "General Introduction, Christian Initiation," Liturgy Office England and Wales, 1985, no. 3, https://www.liturgyoffice.org.uk/Resources/Rites/CIGI.pdf.

The statement that holiness is required of all, regardless of state or walk of life, includes the most skilled and the most dependent members of society and everyone in between. It includes children beyond the age of reason, people in the prime of life, and those degrading from injury or illness who are a shadow of their former selves. This call to holiness includes lawyers and nurses, firefighters and accountants, retirees and residents of adult communities and nursing homes. No one is excluded from perfecting themselves, which means learning to love as God loves. To do this is to share in the divine nature and the fullness of Christian life.

If our goal is to enter the Kingdom of God and partake of the Beatific Vision, we need to approach our deaths accordingly. We should think of it as a two-step process. The first step is to get into the state of grace, which is very easy to do, even on your deathbed, if you are properly disposed. The ease with which this can be accomplished is a sign of God's mercy and His desire to have us come home to Him, where we will find happiness.

If you are not already baptized into Christ, you need to do this. Jesus described Himself as the only way to the Father, and He established the Church as His Body on earth to show us the way home, where Jesus is with the Father until the Last Day. It is not a good idea to put Baptism off, because death can come at any time, ending our opportunity to state our intentions to join with God, which is the purpose of our lives to begin with and the only way to true happiness. If you are unsure whether to believe this, you owe it to yourself to at least visit your local Catholic church and sign up for RCIA (Rite of Christian Initiation of Adults) classes. These are designed to allow interested parties to explore the Catholic Faith, teaching doctrine (what we believe) and practices (how we demonstrate it) in a safe and commitment-free environment.

If we have fallen from grace through mortal sin, we need to partake of the sacrament of Reconciliation. Do not hesitate even if you have not been to Confession since your first one forty years ago. One very good man I know was in this predicament and went to Confession with a list of sins over forty years in the making. He described how cathartic the process was for him—and it will be for you, too. Imagine the weight of forty years of sins expunged in a few moments, opening up Heaven for you. It is an amazingly emotional moment to be freed like this, one that will probably move you to tears. Do not worry about saying the wrong words or not knowing the process anymore. The priests are happy to see people saved, and they will help you through it.

Once in the state of grace, we must strive to share in the divine nature, to love God with such intensity that we have absolutely no tendency to sin, because there will be no sin in Heaven. When we are faced with a limited lifetime due to a terminal injury or illness, the secret is to collect the only currency that transcends death: love. This currency will give you entrance into God's Kingdom, a place to which you could not gain admittance with a billion dollars in gold, diamonds, or bonds—unless, of course, you convert your earthly wealth into love. How is this done? Were the Beatles wrong when they sang that money can't buy love? No, they were not wrong. All the money in the world cannot buy the love of someone else (Song of Sol. 8:7). But you can show your love with money if you spend it for the good of another with no expectation of compensation.

This is pure charity, which is giving lovingly to another, and in the eyes of God, it does not matter whether you give a dollar or a million dollars. What matters is the love you show. The financially secure have no advantage in this. After all, in Mark's Gospel, Jesus noted that the poor widow who gave only a few small coins had given more than the rich people who had given large sums out of their surplus. Why? Because she gave of her livelihood and would be suffering for the benefit of others because of her seemingly modest gift (12:41–44).

Receiving love does not generate the spiritual merit that giving love does. Here, it surely is better to give than to receive. Using your fame, power, or money to help the less fortunate is good, certainly providing a better legacy than visiting all fifty states or climbing the top ten peaks in North America or any of the other personal experiences that people have on their "bucket lists" to do before they die. But better than that is giving of yourself, being willing to sacrifice and suffer for the benefit of another or for the common good. This is giving love redemptively, which is to love as Jesus loved, the highest and most powerful form of love and the one that accrues fastest of all.

Note that intentions matter. If you do good things for a bad reason, the entire action is corrupted and is evil. In Matthew 6, Jesus explains that when people give alms, fast, or pray to be seen and adored by the crowds, they will get no heavenly credit, because they already received the reward they sought (6:1–4, 5–8, 16–18). Instead, choose to do good out of love for God and your neighbor in silence—then God, who sees everything, will repay you, hopefully, with entrance into His Kingdom.

Each of us was made perfectly for our specific roles in God's plan, and God will provide the resources and create the opportunity for us to be successful in our roles if we are willing to follow Him. Remember, it will be in carrying out this role that we will most easily perfect ourselves and become holy. So do not be jealous of someone who may have been given more skills and a bigger role than you. After all, Jesus told us that more will be expected from those who were given more (Luke 12:48). And in the parable of the talents, He made it abundantly clear that everyone was expected to use productively what gifts they had, even the one who was given a single talent to work with (Matt. 25:14-30). When we try to fulfill a role other than the one we are made for, we live a lie and disadvantage ourselves in comparison to the people who were really made for this role. This can also very easily cause people to sin as they struggle to try to compensate for what they naturally lack.

Some roles are huge and last a lifetime, while others are to perform a single action or say the right thing at the right moment in someone else's life. Every role is important, however, because everything and everyone is interconnected; God has seen fit in His wisdom to give us all skill and resource gaps, which we need other people to fill to be successful.

In addition, we all have many roles that utilize and grow different aspects of our being. Our careers and vocations are not always our most important roles. Sometimes our jobs are just the means of providing a livelihood while our more important roles (parent, child, sibling, friend, coach, teacher, and so forth) are done out of love, not for money. The more well-rounded we are, the less susceptible we will be to despair if we lose one of our roles. Importantly, we will feel fulfilled and energized when we take on the roles meant for us, and there will be an emptiness and an urge to change if we take on roles that do not fit our skills. This is because doing God's will leads to happiness and God alone satisfies (CCC 1718).[8] In any case, if we do our activities with love, they will alleviate or avoid suffering, while if we do not act out of love, our activities will cause someone to suffer, probably but not definitively, including ourselves.

Jesus began the Sermon on the Mount, His great summation of His moral teaching, with the eight Beatitudes, which represent the characteristics of Christ and are thus a blueprint for partaking of the divine nature (CCC 1721).[10] They present different ways to love, and when mapped onto any activity, they provide guidance on how to perform that activity with love. Ultimately, the goal is to share in God's nature so we can also share in His life (CCC 1722).[11] A good exercise is to map the Beatitudes onto your activities to see how you can better approach them. As an example, a nurse might look at her career and recognize that to be poor in spirit, her motivation should be not just to make a living but to alleviate suffering. When a nurse puts others' needs before her own, she is practicing meekness. She mourns when expressing empathy for her patients, and by being impartial in her care and not holding a patient's prior actions against him, she demonstrates righteousness and mercy. Similarly, she acts as a peacemaker when she helps mediate conflicts between patients and their doctors. And when she advocates for her patients, even if doing so could hurt her career or her working relationships, she shows her willingness to be persecuted for the sake of righteousness. This exercise, to see how we can live out the Beatitudes in each of our roles, adds structure to the question "What would Jesus do?" and leads us to avoid sin and stay in the state of grace.

Another point to consider is that even with a terminal diagnosis, we can and should try to lead a fulfilling life with the remainder of our time. Our "bucket lists" should consist of doing things that make a difference in people's lives, not in collecting things or experiences that will be totally inconsequential to anyone when we are dead. A few kind words spoken to a stranger will leave a better legacy than going to every state or climbing every mountain. Pass on what you have learned in life in whatever venues you have to whoever can benefit. A gift thoughtfully given, a word kindly spoken, can change a life and help save a soul. If by your words and example you can help save the soul of anyone around you, that is a legacy worth having, even if no one on earth knows of it.

As I touched on previously, we need to love others to stay in the state of grace. One way for the terminally ill to love those around them is to not incessantly talk about dying but instead focus on the activities and plans of our survivors. Most people we meet will not have a need or desire to hear about our ailments, so we should spare them of that and talk about things they are interested in. We will need to discuss our situations with our caregivers, so they know how to best help us and to understand what activities we are capable of. Living people want to talk about life, not death, so if we speak only about our upcoming deaths, we might find ourselves social outcasts.

This can be very hard since our natural tendency is to socialize our ailments so that we do not feel like outsiders. We look for sympathy because what we are going through is hard, and if other people recognize our struggles, we remain a part of the community, reducing the isolation. In truth, though, we are in fact sharing our pain with others against their will. If they ask us seriously about how we are doing, then we can be free to tell them. Better yet is to have someone with a similar problem to commiserate with.

It is also natural for our loved ones, particularly those who are dependent on us, to feel like we are not doing enough to stay alive, especially if we go the hospice path. They may check up on our eating, drinking, and exercise habits, stating, or at least insinuating, that we are not doing enough. Do not correct them and do not be angry with them; remember, they are worried about losing us and all we bring to the family. Instead, listen to their fears. Try to mitigate their worries and deepen your empathy for them by placing yourself in their shoes to consider what it is like to lose someone important.

Living with a degenerative terminal disease can be confusing because it changes your focus and your capabilities over time, which affects the roles you can fill. When you are first diagnosed, you likely are still doing what you did when you were fully healthy. Over time, however, activities and pastimes that you love become increasingly difficult to do, to the point that you eventually find it impossible to carry them out. For instance, I played ultimate frisbee and softball until I could not run without falling down, until I could no longer judge a fly ball, until I could not get up off the ground without great effort or aid. I probably played longer than I should have, but I love those sports, and the only reason I would be willing to give them up was that it was really obvious I could not compete and was hurting my team by continuing to play.

On August 28, 2021, I wrote a blog post, "God Works in Mysterious Ways," in which I discussed how building a deck on my house was positively affecting my mental and physical health. At the time of the blog post, I had been working on the deck for a month, roughly the same time that I had been in physical therapy for Parkinson's disease. Although I was aching every day, the physical therapists were measuring my strength and balance while noting greater than normal improvements, which we all agreed was the result of the extra exercise that came from the building of the deck. My neurologist was "all in," suggesting that I hire myself out to neighbors for deck-building projects when I completed my own. I boldly declared that even chronic degenerative diseases could be turned back, if only the person was motivated to work hard to overcome it. As I transitioned from summer to fall, my enthusiasm was soaring. That was about the time that things started to change.

I went from summer break to the fall semester, teaching two freshman Scripture classes, running the sixth-grade CCD program at St. Agnes Parish, and teaching a course based on *Why All People Suffer* for fifty-three students in the Avila Institute's School of Spiritual Formation that ran on Tuesdays from 8:30 to 10:00

p.m. The Avila schedule was especially tough, made necessary by the class's worldwide reach. Finally, I wanted to write blog posts and magazine articles to support the book, since my publisher's marketing moved to new releases. Physical therapy ended about this time, as did framing the deck, the creative aspect of the deck-building process. What was left was pulling off the old, rotting deck boards, which required strength; putting on the decking material, which required handling twelve- and sixteen-foot-long composite decking boards that were generally too heavy for me; and screwing in thirty-eight hundred screws at foot level, which killed my back.

Although I dearly loved these activities, in combination they were too much for my current capability. But I did not want to give up any of these cherished roles, so I found it very hard to dis-engage from doing things that had previously caused me pleasure. I asked my Parkinson's specialist about the signs I should look for in deciding when I could no longer carry out specific activities like teaching or building decks, and he said, "I don't want you to stop any of it, because once you stop doing these things, you will degrade rapidly." This caused me to pause and contemplate my situation and that of my ninety-year-old mother.

My mother, recently deceased, had been a widow for ten years. During that time, my younger brother Richard was her one con-stant, living with her and caring for her needs at the expense of carrying on his own life. When I moved to Washington in 2015, Rich and I merged our funds to buy a house in Arlington, Virginia, and had a bedroom suite built for our mother on the first floor. For two years, Rich, my wife Sue, and I shared the load of caring for my mother. At that time, my mom could move around with a walker, and although the doctors told us she had dementia, she possessed her full communication skills. She was a bowler in the years after the children left the house, and we introduced her to

Wii bowling, which she loved to play. I enjoyed it too, so we played every night after dinner. Occasionally, someone else would join us.

I had a rule with my mom that if we were going to play the game, we each had to stand when it was our turn because it gave us both at least some exercise. The in-home physical therapist that Medicaid provided, but my mom rebuffed, had a simple statement she used to try to motivate my mom, a statement we also adopted: "Use it or lose it." This pattern of standing while playing went on for the better part of a year, at which point my mom abruptly informed me she was going to play Wii bowling sitting down because standing was becoming too much of a burden. For a few days, I refused to play with her sitting down. I eventually relented and we went back to playing, but she never stood again. In fact, as much as we serenaded her with "use it or lose it," she had made up her mind that the physical suffering from standing was just too much to endure, and her legs became locked at sixty-five-degree angles so she could not stand if she wanted to. Nor could she easily sit in a chair or lay flat, because she could neither flex her legs nor straighten them.

Like my mother, I have had to heed my suffering and stop doing an activity I love because I can no longer take the associated suffering. Now I realize that people who have not reached this stage cannot appreciate just how much it must hurt to willingly give up a beloved activity. I must admit to myself that I misunderstood my mother to be weak when she was actually heeding her suffering and moving on to something else. In her case, I am not sure what she moved on to, but I have faith it was somehow part of God's plan and that it leads to some spiritual growth for someone, maybe me. It is certainly a cautionary tale that we can all learn from.

I must also admit that when I started writing, I was thinking the lesson learned from the deck work was that when the suffering becomes unbearable, it is signaling that we must stop whatever is causing the suffering. But a few more visits with my mom in the assisted-living center dissuaded me from stopping anything without carefully considering the unintended consequences of the decision. While it is doubtful that I will build another deck, I realize I need to replace the movements involved with another form of exercise, or I, too, will lose the ability to stand and all that goes with it. I now understand that suffering and pain will moderate my activity, but the more I push back against it, the longer I will be able to contribute to society and maintain my independence. Also, I understand I do not have enough motivation to push through the pain based on this realization alone, because exercising in pain is drudgery. I need a way to make it fun or at least productive, like building the deck, to keep me motivated to exercise.

This got me thinking about how we judge the right time to abandon roles we love and to move ourselves to the end stage. I now believe that this should be done gradually, by replacing abandoned roles with new ones that fit our new reality. For instance, I can no longer play softball or ultimate frisbee, but I can play Ping-Pong and board games and I can walk for exercise. I will not be able to build a seventy-five-hundred-square-foot two-story deck again, but I can build shelves to give us storage space, and I can also help my children design and build decks and shelves for their own homes in the future, thus passing on the skills as my own father and grandfather did.

Family roles change with time. When my children were young, I was their caregiver and guardian. That role has faded away with the passing years: they are all independent now, with no need of a caregiver or guardian, and, in fact, are becoming caregivers and guardians of their own children. I can see we are now in a transitional set of roles, where we take care of each other in our own ways.

I provide advice and financial support when asked, and they take care of me physically when I need it. Most of my needs, however, are met by my wife, who fortunately is extremely strong, healthy, capable, and loving. I try to do the same in return for her, but at this point, she can help me physically more than I can help her and we have both accepted this new reality, for which I am grateful.

The part that should not change with the changing of roles over time is the love between family members, with each looking out for the best interests of the others, no matter who is cast in the role of caregiver. This is the way God designed the human race, with natural bonds between family members and co-dependencies that are critical to the growth and maintenance of all family members in every generation. Nevertheless, it remains important to acknowledge the contributions of each family member so no one feels used or unappreciated. The natural nuclear family is, after all, the bedrock on which all societies are built, and it is critical to their success.

One of the realities of the human condition is that our bodies degrade over time. Of necessity, that degradation causes those of us whose lives are not cut short by disease and injury to eventually experience physical suffering. We must remember this is part of God's plan of providence and serves several useful purposes, even for the people experiencing excruciating, unrelenting pain. The most important of these is that the pain is a vivid reminder that we are mortal and, as much as we dislike the message, we do not control our own destinies. This focuses our attention on attaining spiritual growth so we can share in the divine nature and life. No matter how rich or powerful we are on earth, nothing stops the rampages of time. Some will undoubtedly argue that the wealthy can afford expensive treatments that mitigate the pain, and this is true, to a point. But medicine has its limits, and no amount of money will ward off death, which, as I discussed earlier, is a critical part of God's plan.

In the end, we need to recognize that as long as we can generate love with our actions, they are worth doing, because we are working as part of the Body of Christ. By doing His will, our loving actions enhance the lives of others while building up spiritual merit for us. When we have completed our part of the plan, God will call us home.

Even as residents in a nursing home or assisted-living community, we can love others and make a difference in their lives. This is true for the fully capable residents as well as the most dependent. Indeed, the most capable can help the less capable in so many ways. Years ago, my great-uncle, Adrian Gastonguay, would help pass out Communion and talk to the other residents in his Massachusetts nursing home, and many others do the same. Most recently, in the peak of the COVID-19 pandemic, my mother's assisted-living community was locked down for the protection of its patients, but that also isolated them from their families, leaving many, like my mother, alone in their rooms for several months. Kathy, one of her fellow residents, saw the situation and took it upon herself to read to my mother every day, a kindness that was noted by our family and the staff. The most dependent, like my mother at the end, can pray for and show appreciation for those who care for them. We are not to stop our efforts until death, and assuming we do not go to Hell, we can pray for the intentions of our loved ones even after death. This is called the communion of saints.

Chapter 13

Planning for Life after Death

Because no one knows the time or form of their death until it happens, it is prudent to always be prepared for what happens after death, both for our eternal souls and for the benefit of those we leave behind. In fact, the two cannot be fully separated, because failure to provide for our dependents is a failure to love, which could have eternal implications for us. There are seven topics to consider when planning for what happens leading up to and following one's death.

1. *The state of your soul.* As previously discussed, we must die in the state of grace to enter the Kingdom of God, so it is important to receive God's grace through Baptism and to avoid mortal sin after that. If we fall from grace through sin, we must partake of the sacrament of Reconciliation to return to grace. If this is not physically possible, or just was not done and you realize you are about to die, the only remaining option is to offer your contrition to God. Contrition is "sorrow of the soul and detestation for the sin committed, together with the resolution not to sin again" (CCC 1451). "When it arises from a love by which God is loved above all

else, contrition is called 'perfect' (contrition of charity). Such contrition remits venial sins; it also obtains forgiveness of mortal sins if it includes the firm resolution to have recourse to sacramental confession as soon as possible" (CCC 1452). If you have the presence of mind to die with perfect contrition in mind, or, better yet, the last thing spoken is to appeal to God's mercy while feeling perfect contrition, then at least you put yourself in roughly the state St. Dismas was in when he made such an appeal to Jesus as both were dying on their crosses on Calvary. Luke tells us Jesus' response to him was "Amen, I say to you, today you will be with me in Paradise" (Luke 23:43).

2. *Resolving relationship issues.* The second consideration is to address any issues with family members or neighbors, be they debts or disagreements. Address them as soon as possible; do not let problems linger out of love for the other party and in recognition that we do not know the time of our deaths. People will not be able to resolve any issues with you when you are dead, so to give them an opportunity is a great mercy.

3. *Provide for our dependents.* The third consideration is to provide as best we can for those who are dependent on us. This includes arranging for suitable guardians for any dependent minor children or adult dependents and documenting your decisions in a will (make sure the designees agree and provide funds for support if you can—be very clear about what funds are for use in supporting the dependent and what funds are available for the dependent alone to use once reaching adulthood or declared competent). This should be done as soon

as possible after you have a dependent and updated as necessary.

4. *Define medical direction.* The fourth point involves getting the care we want if we are not competent to make a call. There are generally two ways to accomplish this. The first is through an advance directive, where we write down what we want to happen under various scenarios and provide it to the individual medical providers who might give us care. The second is to name a surrogate to make those decisions for us. Most localities have statutes that provide our next of kin (however the community defines that) with surrogate power if we do not name a medical power of attorney to the individual medical providers who might give us care. If we file an advance directive, it will supersede any view of the surrogate, because it is your direct statement and autonomy is respected in the law and the medical community.

If you have a trusted surrogate that knows your preferences as I do with my wife, it is better to forgo the advance directive because the surrogate will be able to assess the exact situation better than you will be able to predict the future scenario when writing up the directive. The decision would be different in the absence of a trusted surrogate who is easily contacted, because if medical providers do not have a directive or a surrogate, then they will default to what the institution considers best practice. If you are not being treated by Catholic healthcare services and are not clear in your directions, you or your loved one may be subjected to procedures that are unethical in the eyes of the Church. To help navigate this, several dioceses have put together advice packages and made them available online.[92]

5. *Asset disbursal.* A will should be written and beneficiaries named on all financial accounts as soon as a person is a functioning adult, responsible for their own upkeep, and certainly no later than when they are married and have people dependent on them. Note that beneficiaries should be put on all financial accounts because that puts them outside the probate system, reducing cost, time, and effort on the part of the recipients and the executor of your estate. It is also important to keep an up-to-date record of accounts that your survivors have access to.

6. *Passing on special knowledge.* If you possess special knowledge that is appropriate to pass on (family secrets, recipes, location of your financial accounts, Internet passwords, and so forth), make sure it is properly documented and placed where it can be found (ideally, you tell someone about it, so they can find it). Keep this up to date.

7. *Funeral plans.* If you have specific funeral or burial plans, then make the necessary arrangements and let your survivors know. However, memorials are for those left behind to remember you, so it is appropriate that the survivors make the plans for what will give them comfort. When you move on to the next life, this is unlikely something you will care about, but your survivors might.

People who wait until they are terminally ill to begin working on these seven topics are unlikely to complete them all. It is really

---

[92] This one from my diocese is a good example: https://www.arlingtondiocese.org/uploadedfiles/cda/pages/family_life/family_life/advance%20medical%20directive_english_fillable(1).pdf.

hard to do this when significantly ill and quite possibly impaired. However, if you have not yet completed these tasks when given a terminal diagnosis, then you should be highly motivated to begin. When we recognize our suffering as terminal, we need to switch our priority to planning for our deaths. Ideally this has been ongoing for months, if not years, so it is a matter now of doing final updates. Planning for our death is ultimately more productive at the end-of-life stage than trying to preserve life in a body that is rapidly breaking down, but it is really hard to motivate yourself to do so without terminal suffering to drive home the point that your forthcoming death is actually going to happen. At the same time, it is important for our surviving loved ones that we are diligent about preparing them for our deaths.

The final activity for dying people is to prepare ourselves and those that depend on us for our impending death. When we believe we are facing death, it sparks thoughts of what we want to do with our remaining time. Prudently, the most important prep work we can do is to reconcile with God, sacramentally if possible. This has eternal consequences, so nothing should delay this activity. If Catholic, you should go to Confession and make it a habit to attend Mass as often as possible, certainly on any Sunday or holy day. You should also avail yourself of the sacrament of the Anointing of the Sick and take actions to live your best life as described in the previous chapter.

To have the time and the capability to reconcile with God in our last days is a very great blessing, and it is a shame if it is not acted upon. God is like the father in the parable of the Prodigal Son (Luke 15:11–32), waiting for us to come home to Him with open arms. He has established the sacraments as the way to signal our desire to unite with Him. The most obvious one is Baptism, which makes us members of Christ's Body, His Church. For the already baptized who have fallen away, the defining step is going through the sacrament of Reconciliation (Confession). Ideally, this step should already be in place and this final push is just maintenance.

For those who have been sacramentally cleansed by either of the two aforementioned sacraments, Anointing of the Sick can be most helpful at the end of life. It is focused not on the healing of the body but on the healing of the soul. The *Catechism* says, "The first grace of this sacrament is one of strengthening, peace and courage to overcome the difficulties that go with the condition of serious illness or the frailty of old age" (CCC 1520). It further states that "just as the sacraments of Baptism, Confirmation, and the Eucharist form a unity called 'the sacraments of Christian initiation,' so too it can be said that Penance, the Anointing of the Sick and the Eucharist as viaticum constitute at the end of Christian life 'the sacraments that prepare for our heavenly homeland'" (CCC 1525).

In tandem with this, we need to reconcile with anyone with whom we are still in conflict, out of love for them, since there will be no way for them to resolve the anger or resentment once we are gone. This should be done as expediently as possible since we do not know the day or hour of our passing. Out of love for our survivors, we need to train replacements or leave written directions on activities and processes that only we currently provide but that they will want or need after we are gone. This could be a favorite family recipe or where the tax records are. Disbursal of personal goods can take place as you see fit, but you should not give away things you need for everyday life, because you need to keep on living until God calls you home. At a minimum, you should have a will directing the placement of your assets; but, if possible, you should physically give them away prior to dying, not only to save thousands in taxes but also because you can convey the meaning behind your gift to your survivors in a way that a sterile document would not, and it would be better appreciated. Also, share with the recipients the location of your online and physical accounts, insurance, brokerages, and any other assets you have that can be claimed. If you have brokerage accounts, it is better to have the beneficiary information updated than to disburse them with the will, which would probably drive your survivors into probate court.

If you have work that others do not do and that you would like to have continued after your passing, you need to train one or more backups and retire or work as a master of the house, delegating your projects to others. If you hold the inner workings of your projects "close to the vest," that is where they will end up: with you in the casket, where they will not help anyone. As a last measure of your love for your survivors, make it as easy as possible for them to succeed. If you do this well, you will have left two legacies: the project and your replacement.

It is important that as we feel ourselves dying, we consciously prioritize how we spend our last days and weeks. It requires balance between treating the terminal disease, living our normal lives, and planning for our deaths. We need to treat the disease enough to keep us functional to complete our other activities. But we also need to continue meeting our responsibilities to others, and, for both ourselves and our survivors, we need to update and firm up our plans for after our death.

Section III

Dealing with the Dying
and Death of Loved Ones

Chapter 14

The Suicide of a Loved One

Suicide results when a person is more afraid of suffering than of death. Because of the strength of the desire for self-preservation, suicide is unusual (1.5 percent of all deaths) and abnormal (linked to mental illness).[93] There are two distinctly different types of suicides. One type, which we already discussed in chapter 11, is that of a terminally ill patient who wants to take control over his destiny. In this situation, if you are a close associate or family member, you probably have advance warning of the event and should take the opportunity to try and dissuade them of this course of action, both for the negative implications to the survivors such as yourself and for their eternal souls. If you have done this and they proceed anyway, remember that everyone has free will and there is only so much we can do to change anyone's mind about anything. Also, we can never judge the person, because we do not have the full insight into the situation that God does.

[93] World Health Organization, "2019: Estimated Deaths." Mental illness is a major risk factor for suicide. The World Health Organization estimates that 90 percent of all suicide victims have some kind of mental health condition—often depression or substance abuse.

The second type of suicide involves a person, too often in her teens or early adulthood, who is overwhelmed with things going on in her life and decides to just end it. These suicides are simply tragic for the survivors, because they are usually unexpected and leave a gaping hole in our lives. Our first thought may be to worry about the status of our loved one's soul. Recognizing God's abundant mercy, the Church teaches that "we should not despair of the eternal salvation of persons who have taken their own lives. By ways known to him alone, God can provide the opportunity for salutary repentance. The Church prays for persons who have taken their own lives" (CCC 2283). In addition, realizing the potential for extenuating circumstances, the Church teaches that "grave psychological disturbances, anguish, or grave fear of hardship, suffering, or torture can diminish the responsibility of the one committing suicide" (CCC 2282).

Suicide is particularly stressful for the survivors, who inevitably wonder what drove the person to suicide and whether they missed some signal that would have allowed them to give the suicidal person a reason to live. Sometimes, survivors will successfully identify the factor that caused such extreme suffering in a person's life that it overrode the innate instinct to preserve one's life. The best of these survivors will work to eradicate these factors so that others do not share in their pain.

John Halligan was a co-worker thirty years ago. In 2003, his thirteen-year-old son, Ryan, committed suicide after extensive cyberbullying, which only became apparent after the fact by going through his computer records. Mason[94] had physically and

[94] Mason and Ainsley are not the real names of those involved with Ryan Halligan's suicide. John Halligan gave them theses names to protect their identities.

emotionally bullied Ryan since fifth grade, making fun of his learning disability and telling his classmates that Ryan was gay. Ainsley, a girl he liked, led him on and then humiliated him in public, calling him a loser that no one would go out with. Others taunted him online, telling Ryan he was a loser and that he should kill himself, sending him links on how to do so.

Early in the morning of October 7, 2003, Ryan's seventeen-year-old sister found him hanging from the shower rod. John, who was away from home on business, was absolutely devastated by his son's suicide, which he writes about very poignantly in his book, *Ryan's Story*.[95] John's description of his thoughts and emotions as he struggled to get back to his family and to come to grips with the cause of Ryan's angst should be required reading for anyone contemplating suicide to demonstrate the effects of their action on their survivors. Ryan's death devastated not only his family but also Ainsley, whom he had told the day before, "It's girls like you that make me want to kill myself." Mason, on the other hand, continued to bully Ryan, now dead, telling his classmates that "Ryan was weak. He couldn't handle life and he was gay."

When John heard that Ainsley was being harassed by classmates and had become suicidal herself, he called her mother and invited her and Ainsley to his home to discuss the situation. When they came over, he took Ainsley by the hand and said to her, "Ainsley, you did a mean thing, but I do not believe for a second that you are a mean person or that you would have done what you did if you knew Ryan would do what he did. This is not your fault." He followed up by telling the parents of his son's friends that his

[95] John P. Halligan with Emily B. Dickson, *Ryan's Story: A Father's Hard-Earned Lessons about Cyberbullying and Suicide* (self-pub., 2019), ISBN: 978-0-578-42942-7.

family had met with Ainsley and did not believe Ryan's death was her fault. He then asked them to ask their sons to defend her if others harassed her about her role in Ryan's suicide.

When John heard that Mason continued to harass Ryan even after his death, he went to his home and asked to talk to his parents and to him. John told Mason, "You probably have no idea. You probably have no idea, the amount of pain you created in my son's life. So much pain because of you and your friends who decided to bully my son, since the fifth grade, about the two issues he struggled with for most of his life. And I just received this phone call tonight, and I'm finding out that you are continuing to bully my son. My son who is no longer here to even defend himself."

When Mason denied it, John told him, "You're lying to me and you're lying to your parents right now. But you know what? I refuse to believe that you are that heartless; I refuse to believe that you are that empty of a soul. I think you are just a dumbass thirteen-year-old, trying to act tough, trying to keep this stupid bully reputation going on at the middle school. But I refuse to believe that you are this heartless." Mason began to sob and apologized profusely.

John did what Ryan was ill-prepared or suited to do: he let Mason and Ainsley see his vulnerability and how they had hurt Ryan, giving them a chance for repentance and redemption. This was truly an act of love where others would have sought revenge from people who had caused him and his family so much pain, and it is a great example of how to deal with those who persecute or oppress us.

John Halligan quit his tech sector job and started a ministry addressing cyberbullying in middle schools across the country. He has told Ryan's story, in person, to over 1 *million* students in school assemblies since 2004. He wrote *Ryan's Story* in 2019 and self-published it as a way to augment his in-person presentations.[96] Ryan's story has several important messages. God did not will Ryan to commit suicide; that was the result of sin on the part of all his antagonists and also Ryan himself, who gave up hope in God's goodness. Ryan was hurt by the bullying, but that does not make his action a moral one, just an understandable one. We cannot judge Ryan, or anyone else for that matter, because we do not have all the information. One thing we know is that a mortal sin requires grave matter that is undertaken with full understanding and full consent. Suicide is clearly grave matter, but Ryan was being harassed, so he probably did not fully consent to his actions, and it is also questionable whether his mind was clear enough to have full understanding of the implication of his actions.[97] We know God can read our hearts and souls and can accurately judge whether Ryan was fully culpable for a mortal sin or not. But even if He found Ryan culpable, He could do what the Church suggests: "By ways known to him alone, God can provide the opportunity for salutary repentance" (CCC 2283). In Ryan's particular case, perhaps God gave him a glimpse of the effect of his actions on those that loved him, causing him to seek reconciliation with God and entrance into His Kingdom. Such an action could be part of Purgatory, where we will be purified and taught to love divinely

---

[96] John P. Halligan with Emily B. Dickson, *Ryan's Story: A Father's Hard-Earned Lessons about Cyberbullying and Suicide* (self-pub., 2019), ISBN:978-0-578-42942-7.

[97] World Health Organization, "2019: Estimated Deaths." Mental illness is a major risk factor for suicide. The World Health Organization estimates that 90 percent of all suicide victims have some kind of mental health condition—often depression or substance abuse.

through suffering, filling in any gaps left by the four tasks of suffering on earth.

John's actions are an example of God turning evil into good, as his ministry has given him closure, has educated over a million students on how to deal with bullying, and brought him back to the practice of his faith. He is a shining example of how to respond to the tragedy of suicide with love.

Note that I knew the vague details of John's story but did not include it in my first book. I had not seen John in close to thirty years, but he responded to an early entry of mine on LinkedIn, advocating for people to buy my book before he even read it. I sent him an electronic copy (it had not been published yet) and, having become aware that he had published a book, ordered it and found that his work was an exceptional response to an extremely difficult situation. We have been conversing regularly for the past year, helping each other out as much as possible, and the relationship has become a true blessing.

Chapter 15

The Unexpected Death
of a Loved One

The unexpected death of a loved one is the hardest for people to deal with, particularly when the person is in seemingly good health and there was no warning to prepare the survivors. The more involved this person was in your life, the bigger the void that needs to be filled when he is not there to fill it. The instantaneous emergence of these voids makes them harder to fill immediately, leaving you with many potential questions. It will be natural to question why the person was taken from you, to wonder what happens to him now, to worry what or who is going to fill those gaps in your life.

To try to answer these questions generically, God controls the universe and God loves us all. There is a reason every person dies. It is never truly random or meaningless. People who die without warning are spared terminal suffering, but at the same time, they lack its warning. For the diligent and devout, who live in the state of grace, a quick, relatively painless death is a blessing. The survivors, too, can be comforted by the relative lack of suffering in these unexpected deaths, which are most often the result of a heart attack, a stroke, a traffic accident, drowning, or a fall.[98] As discussed in the last chapter, the suicide of a loved one will usually be unexpected by the survivors.

Like John Halligan, the people left behind after an unexpected death may be very anxious to make sense of it and may find some solace advocating for changes that will save others from the same fate. People whose loved ones die in traffic fatalities will sometimes mark the spot with a memorial, which at least for a time will identify the scene as dangerous. Those whose loved ones die of a heart attack or stroke may request donations to the associations that look for cures for these diseases, in lieu of flowers at the funeral, and the most motivated will find a role in their support.

Expect the grief and mourning to be more intense for an unexpected death than for a ninety-year-old man who has been through terminal suffering for five years. There are two factors driving this. The first is that the grieving process for the terminally ill person is divided and spread out over the length of his illness, while for the unexpected death, the grief is focused all on the short period in which it becomes public knowledge. The second factor is that the ninety-year-old had time to live to his fullest potential, while the person who died unexpectedly probably did not and that is to be mourned.

There may be a tendency among some to be angry with the victim for abandoning them or with God for taking their loved one from them. This anger is mostly misplaced in terms of the victim and totally misplaced toward God. With the exception of suicide, the victim did not mean to die. However, if he failed to take precautions in dangerous situations and also failed to take the necessary steps to provide for those dependent on him, then

---

[98] World Health Organization, "2019: Estimated Deaths."

they have a valid complaint. But being angry at the dead person will not change anything unless it is used to help others be aware of the needs of dependents when doing financial planning.

At the same time, being angry with God is also misplaced. God is not vengeful and does nothing out of malice. The fact that a loved one's death is surprising to you does not mean that God does not love you or the victim. Perhaps the death was not about you at all but was good for the deceased or some onlooker. It could be that your loved one had fulfilled his part in God's plan and this was the way that God chose to bring the person home. It may be that the person died particularly well, inspiring others to faith. Or maybe the loved one was holding you back in some way that was keeping you from carrying out your role in God's plan. In any case, there are many plausible reasons that a loving God would call a person home at any time—but not one good reason that God would do it in a vindictive way. If you find yourself angry at God for the unexpected loss of a loved one, consider the ways that this might help you, the deceased, or someone else get to Heaven.

Also have faith that God will attend to your needs, both terrestrial and eternal, if you follow His lead. It is a good thing that you remember the deceased loved one. Love is eternal currency that cannot be lost or stolen, and it is the only thing you can take with you when you die. Your love will continue after the object of that love is dead, and the person can continue to love you even after death. As St. Paul writes to the Corinthians and to all of us, "Love never fails" (1 Cor. 13:8).

I know that it can be hard to fill the gaps left in our lives by the loss of others. If you had a routine that you shared with the deceased, like walking after dinner, continue the practice in memory of them. You do not need one person to backfill all that the deceased did with and for you. You will not find an exact replica, because everyone is unique and has their own strengths and weaknesses. Instead, expand your existing relationships and make new ones to meet your emotional and social needs.

As for your material needs, follow Jesus' advice from the Sermon on the Mount:

> Do not worry and say, "What are we to eat?" or "What are we to drink?" or "What are we to wear?" All these things the pagans seek. Your heavenly Father knows that you need them all. But seek first the kingdom [of God] and his righteousness, and all these things will be given you besides. Do not worry about tomorrow; tomorrow will take care of itself. Sufficient for a day is its own evil. (Matt. 6:31–34)

Depend on God. You will be surprised and happy with where this leads you. He may allow you to struggle a bit at the beginning to test your resolve, but if you follow where He leads you, avoiding what causes you or others to suffer, I am quite confident that you will like what results.

Chapter 16

The Five Needs of the Terminally Ill

People who are terminally ill have five concerns that they are typically dealing with:
1. Their physical pain
2. Uncertainty about their medical prognosis
3. Concern about their purpose in life
4. Concern about their social status
5. Concern about what will happen after they die (their spiritual status)

The terminally ill patient will generally recognize that they have these concerns in this order, but in reality, the importance is in inverse order. Caregivers will greatly improve a terminally ill person's dying and death if they are attentive to these needs but can also add to the dying person's suffering by being inattentive or unresponsive to her needs.

Spiritual Needs

People who have terminal injuries or illnesses will almost by definition experience their powerlessness, limitations, and finitude as the *Catechism* warns (CCC 1500). While injuries and illnesses can lead to anguish, self-absorption, and even revolt against God, they can also be catalysts for conversion. To feed that conversion, a caregiver needs to provide for catechesis and access to the sacraments.

This task is the most important job of the caregiver because this is the last opportunity for the dying to reconcile with God. To not provide them with the information they need to find God in their suffering—or worse, to deny them access to the sacraments—is a dereliction of duty and a tragedy of the greatest magnitude.

Social Status

Humans are social creatures by design, and people struggle to find their roles in society. Caregivers must help terminally ill patients maintain their place in society. This can be done by keeping patients informed of activities and news of their social groups, arranging for visitation with friends and family, and making patients feel wanted and loved. One goal of the dying patient should be to reconcile with anyone they are estranged from. They will need to have the caregiver's aid in contacting and meeting with these people. If, on the other hand, the caregiver isolates the patient from peers and family or makes the patient feel like a burden, then the patient will suffer tremendous psychological and social wounds.

Sense of Purpose

Humans need to feel they have a reason to exist and that they are fulfilling their purpose. With this in mind, caregivers should help patients see how their lives can have meaning, even with a terminal illness. Caregivers can also point out that even the most dependent person can make a difference in the world through prayer and by treating everyone that cares for her with kindness and understanding.

Another very worthwhile activity to enhance a patient's feeling of self-worth is to arrange for the patient to train someone on tasks they feel are important to hand down so they will not be lost with their death or descent into dementia. This can range from passing down the secret family recipes to outlining the research project they were working on. While they are still lucid, get them engaged in passing on their goods and their knowledge. This is an excellent way to give them a purpose that is truly valuable.

On the other hand, the caregiver can also make a patient feel like a burden, which will negatively affect their self-esteem and sense of worth.

Certainty about Their Prognosis

Every person has the need to feel safe as part of the natural instinct to preserve our lives. Patients also have the right to know their own medical status to allow future planning. It is incumbent on the caregiver to find out what can be expected in terms of length and quality of life with various treatment options and to be transparent about sharing the information with the patient. I recommend this with anyone above the age of reason because uncertainty is extremely stressful. My father understood this and required all medical personnel to include me in every discussion on treatment options and prognoses when I was undergoing my second open heart surgery as a teenager. It was a great kindness to me that he did that, although some of the medical personnel may have been uncomfortable going through it with me and answering any questions I had. I felt much more comfortable with the surgery and the aftermath because the surgeon exuded confidence in the procedure and his ability to make me well; he also told me exactly what he was going to do and that the danger of death was, in his words, negligible.

Conversely, if the patient is kept in the dark, she will likely be very uncomfortable, imagining scenarios that are at times worse than reality. Not knowing is worse than a bad prognosis, because at least with a poor prognosis, one can put together a mitigation plan, while all one can do with uncertainty is worry.

Comfort

The final need that caregivers must handle is to provide for patients' comfort and dignity. This is the central concept in hospice and palliative care. Though this is usually the first need the patient is aware of, it has the least lasting effect because it is the easiest to tolerate. In some medical institutions, virtually all discomfort may be treated with sedatives. This option might be particularly tempting in the case of the demented, who can only communicate nonverbally.

However, this is poor care because it robs the patient's consciousness and, with it, her ability to communicate, to contribute in any way to anything. It also does not address the root cause of the problem. People have pain for a reason—it results from wounds or other gaps in bodily integrity. To simply suppress the warning signs means that the actual problem, which goes untreated, will continue to get worse. But by heeding the patient's suffering and addressing its root cause, the caregiver helps the patient and will alleviate the suffering. At the same time, if the caregiver fails to address the root cause, either by ignoring or just masking the pain, it leads to more suffering.

A good caregiver, whether a family member or a professional, is motivated by love, putting the patient's needs above their own. Such a person will seek to always alleviate the patient's suffering. As we have shown above, the caregiver has a strong impact on the patient's comfort and well-being. A big factor in the caregiver's success will be the environment used for the patient's care. Perhaps as a sign of our misplaced priorities, pay rates for professional caregivers are amongst the lowest of any profession, yet caregivers have tremendous influence on the quality of our dying and death.[99] The fact that most of the individuals I have observed in these positions are truly loving people points to the vocational aspects of this type of job, one where the reward is the spiritual merit to be gained from the job and not the pay.

[99] "Salaries by Profession and Industry," Indeed, https://www.indeed.com/career/salaries?from=gnav-title-webapp.

Chapter 17

Choosing a Living Environment
for a Dying Loved One

The first decision that a primary caregiver, typically the closest relative, needs to address is where the person will live out the last days of his life. With this decision come many considerations that must be evaluated on a case-by-case basis. A responsible caregiver will evaluate how best to provide the five basic needs of the dying person. The options available to most people include caring for the person in their own homes themselves; bringing home aides and nurses into the dying person's home; and moving the dying person into an assisted-living community, or a nursing home if they need more medical attention, and finally to the hospital for extensive care needs. These choices represent increasing professional care and, with it, increasing costs.

Most people start off assuming that they would be best served in the comfort of their own home, being under the care of family members. But caring for a senior relative can be incredibly hard, particularly once dementia sets in. At that point, the dying are completely dependent on others to do even the most basic tasks of living, like feeding, going to the toilet, dressing, or moving from place to place. Such a person requires twenty-four-hour-a-day monitoring, which is generally too much to take on for one caregiver. Caregivers who attempt this by themselves will get less sleep than those caring for an infant, because infants get fourteen to seventeen hours of sleep per day while the healthy senior will get half that (seven to eight hours), and various conditions and drug regimens will drive their sleep time below that.[100] Because the terminally ill need continuing care, there is no way to work a separate job, even a remote one, and provide the level of care needed. Caring for a demented senior is a full-time, almost twenty-four-hour-a-day job.

Some people take the home choice and hire a nurse or nurse aide to provide medical care and to give the caregiver a chance to work or do things for themselves or the rest of their families. There are several agencies that provide these services in all major cities and their suburbs. This can work, but it comes at the cost of some inevitable disruption to family routines, even under the best circumstances. It is literally inviting a stranger into your home, with all their idiosyncrasies. It can seem like you are a perpetual host, with no time to relax.

Some caregivers will try to share the burden of caregiving. My family tried this once, but I would not recommend it. My maternal grandfather, Joseph Murdock, became a widower in 1976, when my grandmother died of a stroke. My grandfather did not feel comfortable living alone in a farmhouse in rural Maine, a mile from the nearest neighbor and twenty minutes from the nearest relative, so he moved in with that relative, my uncle Gene and his wife Barbara and their five young children. Caring for my grandfather plus the five children was understandably challenging for them, so they proposed that all four of my grandfather's children

[100] Ryan Fiorenzi, "Sleep Needs by Age and Gender," Start Sleeping, October 5, 2022, https://startsleeping.org/sleep-needs/.

take a turn in caring for him for three months at a time. Everyone agreed that this was fair and that it would give my grandfather a chance to spend time with all his children and grandchildren—and a change in scenery as he migrated from Maine to Hartford to Washington and then Denver.

The plan was made with good intentions, but we found it just did not work. It left my poor grandfather a nomad with no home base and a need to fit into new environments every few months, not an easy task for anyone but I never heard him complain. It also disrupted every home he went to because no one had a spare bedroom, so others had to share. Although he was not demanding, he still needed care and attention in growing households with multiple children, who also needed care and attention. There was also a loss of continuity of his medical care, which becomes important as you age. In short, it met no one's needs and made everyone miserable.

After one rotation, everyone agreed to halt the experiment, and Uncle Gene found an assisted-living community in Maine near his home, where my grandfather lived for the remainder of his life, almost fifteen years. During the last nine of those years, beginning in 1982, after I moved to New York to work, I would drive three hundred miles to Maine once a month to visit my grandfather (and my paternal grandmother, as already discussed). At the beginning we played cribbage and talked about the Red Sox and our relatives, and it was all very pleasant, but over time, he developed dementia and could say nothing at all.

It was my first practical experience with dementia. I sat with him and held a one-sided conversation, not knowing whether he understood what I was saying but hoping it gave him some solace. The home seemed to fit him. He was now living in a community not far from his original home in the kind of rural community that everyone knows a little about everyone else. He seemed content because, unlike during his year of wandering, his five basic needs were being met.

Eventually, home care becomes impractical for all but the most motivated and organized caregivers. It can be a heartrending decision for the caregiver to admit that the care of a spouse or parent is beyond their capability and to seek professional care in an adult or senior living facility. This is not a failure on the part of the caregiver but a prudent choice, if they can find a place that better meets the five needs that all people have. Indeed, in my personal experience, a good assisted-living community will offer solutions for all five needs that would be hard for a relative caregiver to match:

- Physical comfort: they will have a nurse on duty to treat pain, administer medication, and provide restaurant-caliber meals.
- Medical certainty: they all have trained medical staff to cater to residents.
- Social: they will be with peers and can have visitors.
- Purpose: most facilities offer enrichment activities (concerts, plays, daytrips).
- Spiritual needs: the Catholic Church and other religious groups run facilities that are designed specifically to meet the spiritual needs of their residents and their families, but even most secular facilities have pastoral support from local churches for spiritual needs.

The best caregivers will assess each option and find the optimum choice for their loved one. Cost will be a consideration for most people, but there are state and federal programs, including Medicaid, that will help or even assume the cost for eldercare. The facilities themselves will generally help patients get the available government subsidies for their offerings.

If you are in the process of considering assisted living for your loved one, the Elder Care Alliance, an industry group, has helpfully published a list of signs that your parent might need to move to an assisted-living facility, including the following indications that your loved one needs assistance:[101]

- needing reminders to take medication
- noticeable weight loss or gain
- loss of mobility or increase in falls
- signs of neglecting household maintenance
- no longer able to perform daily tasks, such as grooming or preparing meals
- increased isolation
- loss of interest in hobbies

Many elder care communities offer specialized neighborhoods for residents with dementia. Signs that your parent might need memory care include the following:

- exhibiting aggressive behaviors
- becoming disoriented or getting lost
- repeating stories or questions
- problems speaking or struggling to find the right words
- difficulty planning, concentrating, or organizing
- an Alzheimer's or dementia diagnosis or cognitive decline that requires twenty-four-hour supervision

Going to a nursing home or hospital is generally not the dying person's or the caregiver's choice but a medical necessity should they choose to treat their disease aggressively, rather than turning to hospice and accepting their death, or to treat wounds that are

---

[101] "Signs Your Parents May Need Assisted Living," Elder Care Alliance, January 17, 2017, https://eldercarealliance.org/blog/signs-your-parent-may-need-assisted-living/.

beyond the scope of assisted living. These types of facilities exist to treat medical conditions that require around-the-clock nursing and medical care, so the quality of life is much lower than in assisted-living communities. According to one study, the average age of a person who will die in a nursing home is eighty-three, after about fourteen months in the home. Just over half (53 percent) will die within six months of entering such a facility.[102] This is not a matter of poor care in these facilities, but a consequence of their mission to take the patients whose medical conditions are the most challenging and who need the most demanding care.

As I mentioned earlier, my brother Richard and I bought a house in Arlington, Virginia, in August 2015 and had a bedroom suite built on the first floor for our mother, who was eighty-three at that time and had been living with Rich and our sister Maria since the death of my father in 2011. Because Sue, Rich, and I all had day jobs, we hired an aide to sit with our mom during the day. We had three different ones over the two years she stayed with us, and they all were diligent, loving people who tried their best to be unobtrusive to our family while caring for my mother during business hours.

When my mother came to live with us, she was walking with a walker and fully conversant, and although she had been diagnosed with dementia, it was not very obvious. As discussed earlier, she felt pain when standing up, and so she moved to a wheelchair. Her lack of mobility made it impossible for us to leave her alone in the house, and also to move her. She fell once in a diner parking

<hr />

[102] Steve Tokar, "Social Support Is Key to Nursing Home Length of Stay Before Death," Patient Care, University of California San Francisco, October 34, 2010, https://www.ucsf.edu/news/2010/08/98172/social-support-key-nursing-home-length-stay-death.

lot, and we became worried about her safety. All six of her children got together on a conference call, and we agreed that for her own safety and also for enhanced social opportunities, we would investigate moving her into an assisted-living facility. Rich and I scouted out the local options and found three finalists that we presented to our mom.

As the eldest sibling, I was asked to tell our mother of our decision. It was the toughest conversation of my life. As I explained that we felt we could not care for her safely, she kept asking me, "Why do things have to change?" I kept answering that they had already changed, and we were just reacting to them.

We took her to the three finalists, and the director of the third place, Colleen, took my mom by the hand and said to her, "Do not worry, Dolly. I promise you that I will take good care of you. We have many interesting activities, and you will make a lot of new friends." My mom was sold because Colleen made her feel comfortable that she would cover the five needs—and she did, as long as she was director of the facility.

Unfortunately, Colleen left to teach others how to run a facility, and her replacement did not run the facility nearly as well. There was a lot of staff turnover, and care degraded to the point that my mother, who was physically and mentally degrading fairly rapidly, had an accident in which a pitcher of hot water was dumped in her lap, giving her third-degree burns that caused her to spend three weeks at the hospital burn center. When my mother got out of the hospital, the new director refused to let her come back to live in her facility, forcing us to scramble to find a suitable place. Fortunately, I had already investigated new options prior to the accident, and the best of the options had availability only a few weeks later. In the interim, my mother recuperated at a local nursing home, which was dark and dank and unpleasant, causing my mother to dub it the "dungeon."

This highlights three concerns with assisted living. First, the best-run facilities are a function of their directors, and when the directors move on, the facilities may change dramatically—for better or worse. Second, the best-run facilities have long waiting lists, and to get in, you have to be somewhat lucky in needing a room when someone else vacates it. Third, it is very hard to change facilities, not only because of availability of options but because it is expensive to move and disruptive for the residents to leave routines and people they are accustomed to.

A loving caregiver is not necessarily one that does the direct day-to-day care but one who arranges for the best care for his loved one based on the five needs I presented in the last chapter. Recognize, too, that this may require some compromises based on the changing health needs of your loved one. The guiding principle should be the golden rule: Is this the decision you would make for yourself if you were in this situation with these choices? If you can honestly say yes, then your conscience should be clear. If not, you should reconsider your choice.

Chapter 18

Why Did My Innocent Child Die?

The first question someone asked me in the first webinar I did on *Why All People Suffer* was "How could a good God cause or even allow innocent children to suffer with fatal disabilities?" It is the question that drove Rabbi Harold S. Kushner to question the power of God in *When Bad Things Happen to Good People*. While every case has individual characteristics and there are always implications to every event that are beyond our ability to understand, we can at least look at the "Big Picture" and identify plausible reasons that apply generically to cases like these. At the same time, know that we will not be able to identify all the interactions that happen from secondary and tertiary effects on individual cases, because we do not have visibility into all the ways people interact with each other.

We will look at two cases. First, we will look at the death of young children, using Tay-Sachs as the proxy. Included in this case are all people of any age whose mental handicaps make rational thought, and hence the ability to sin, impossible. And then we will look at the death of teenagers who have reached the age of reason and have the potential to sin. We will use progeria, the genetic defect that killed Aaron Kushner, as the proxy. Examining these two cases should provide a means for readers to consider their own specific situations.

Tay-Sachs is a rare inherited lipid metabolism disorder that causes too much of a fatty substance to build up in the brain, a process that begins in the womb.[103] Affected children grow normally for their first six months and then experience progressive loss of mental ability, blindness, deafness, trouble swallowing, seizures, dementia, and death by the age of five, even with the best of care. This disease is extremely harsh, and there remains no cure, so parents, if they have been screening, will often choose to abort the child rather than have her suffer. This is a huge mistake because killing innocent children to save them from suffering is to deny them their mission, which is to help us see what is important in life and to encourage us to take the necessary actions to join God in His Kingdom.

Each one of us was made perfectly by God, for the role He gives us. This is true for innocent children with Tay-Sachs disease as well. Because they will never reach the age of reason, and thus cannot be responsible for mortal sin, these children are all likely to go to Heaven. Like everyone else, their role on earth is to help the people in their lives to get to Heaven as well. And how do they do this? By simply helping those around them love more profoundly, which happens not because the child has outstanding talent but because God gave this specific child to these parents, this family, to care for. Parenthood makes almost everyone a better person because it shifts their center of attention from themselves to their children. This shift increases with the increased attention required

[103] "Tay-Sachs Disease Information Page," Genetic and Rare Diseases Information Center, National Institutes of Health, https://rarediseases.info.nih.gov/diseases/7737/tay-sachs-disease.

for special-needs children. In fact, the parents of a fatally disabled child will progress through all four tasks of suffering with the experience, culminating in redemptive love when they suffer for the benefit of their child. As hard as it is to watch your child suffer, if you hold and comfort her, you reduce the child's suffering while increasing yours, thus sharing in her suffering.

The fact that their lifespans are so short is actually a sign of the mercy of God. Even in a few short years, these children will change the lives of their parents, siblings, and onlookers. In the final analysis, when young children suffer like this for a few years, they open up an eternity of joy for both themselves and those who learn from them what true redemptive love is. When they die, they go to Heaven, having suffered for the benefit of others as Jesus did. There they will wait for us to join them, providing even more impetus for us to focus on spiritual rather than material growth.

This is not to say that everyone with a special-needs child was initially deficient in their capacity to love either God or their children. In fact, one reason the righteous suffer is to provide a model of faithfulness for others who do need to enhance their capacity to love. For an example, read the book of Job in the Bible. As previously discussed, Job was made to suffer because he was the most righteous man on earth, and God needed to use him as an example of faithfulness for the rest of us.

The end result of all this is that the parents and the child will meet in Heaven since they both demonstrated they would suffer for the benefit of the other. The child's suffering is obvious—so obvious that it is hard to watch. Yet the parents do more than just watch: they console the child, thus sharing in the child's suffering. Parents inevitably say that they do not want their children to suffer for their sake, but that just shows that they love their child and that the child succeeded in her role.

The dynamics are a little different when the child survives until the teenage years, like Aaron Kushner. Having achieved the age of reason, these children have the possibility of having mortal sin on their souls as well as the ability to understand that they are going to die. This means that it is incumbent on the parents to prepare the fatally compromised teenager for death. They need to find appropriate catechesis for the dying teenager and give her access to the sacraments. For a teenager, as with an adult, the five needs will be in play, so the parents have to help the teen find purpose in her life and help her connect with people of the same age.

It is absolutely imperative that you communicate their full prognosis so that they understand what they are up against and so they have a reason to contemplate what is important to do. If you can, try to explain why some people, like themselves, are destined to die young. Be sure to emphasize to your child that this is not a punishment and that God is not abandoning her. In fact, it is often just the opposite in cases like these. God may in fact be very pleased with the teen, if she bears her suffering well, willingly doing so for the benefit of others, and because that is redemptive, she is being called home to God. If the teen's presence has made you a better, more loving person, communicate this to them, because it will help them find closure for themselves to know that they carried out the most basic role of all people: to help their loved ones get to Heaven.

Encourage them to participate in church youth groups and hospital groups with people suffering the same fate to help them understand what is happening and what comes next. Set the expectation that you will meet again in Heaven and will get to spend eternity in their company and that you will continue to pray for each other no matter what side of death you are on. There will be occasions when these discussions will be not only appropriate but needed. You will be able to tell when they are thinking about this, but do not make it an everyday topic. Emphasize leading as normal a life as possible, while they still can. Try to give them as normal a childhood as possible so they can have a social life, so they can learn to love and learn how to be a good friend.

When your child dies, be comforted by the fact that God loves them even more than you do. He knows they have suffered, and if they accept that God needed them to sacrifice for the good of others, then He will glorify them and take them into His presence. Trust that from there, they will continue to follow your life on earth and pray for you when you need it so that you can join with them. This should be motive enough to encourage your continued spiritual growth.

Chapter 19

Why Did My Parent Die
When I Was Young?

When parents die when their children are still minors, as harsh as it is on the children, we should assume that it is for the benefit of someone's soul. It could be the parents are being called home because they have fulfilled the role God intended for them, and it could be for the benefit of the children, with God planning for them to be raised by others or to become self-sufficient at an early age. Typically, this is hard to know as it is happening because we have preconceived notions about what we would like our lives to be that cloud our vision. But God's wisdom and the beauty of His plans will become clearer with time, a fact we can have some confidence in by reviewing the results of His plan for previous generations.

My paternal great-grandfather, Alexandre Antoine Chaloux, was born in 1843 just a few miles north of the U.S. border in Paquetteville, Quebec. He was an impressive man, based strictly on the available records. He was a lumber camp boss, managing up to six camps at once for the Van Dyke brothers' logging business, the biggest logging company in the region. They conducted river drives into New Hampshire to sell their wood. He obviously had significant management skills and was respected in the community. He was named an inspector of roads and bridges in 1878 and a town counselor representing the French-speaking residents of Paquetteville in 1891.[104] He was a significant landowner in the town, owning four parcels totaling 310 acres, which he planted with grains like oats and flax. [105]He also managed to father twenty-three children, six by his first wife, Lea Thibault, who in 1882 tragically died at age thirty-two in childbirth along with her sixth child. On October 24, 1883, Alexandre, then a forty-year-old widower with five children, married twenty-one-year-old Exilia Moran, and together over the next twenty years, they had seventeen children with no twins, all but two who lived to adulthood. My grandfather Andre was the last of the births, on May 5, 1903.

Alexandre died on October 29, 1905, when Andre was just two years old. Andre mourned for his whole life the father he never knew, carrying his picture with him until he died, leaving it with me. When Alexandre died, he left Exilia with fifteen minor children (the second family), and five adult children from his first marriage (dubbed the "first family"), without providing for the support of any of them. This was probably due in large part to the relative poverty of the area, which induced most of the family to immigrate to the United States over the next twenty years.

His entire life, my grandfather sought the physical reason for his father's death, but no one seemed to know, or at least no one was willing to talk about it with him. It seems very strange that a man as prominent in the area as he seemed to be, who had two brothers living in the town and a very large immediate family — and

---

[104]Rollande Gendreau, *Paquetteville-St. Venant 1862–1987* (Paquetteville, Quebec, 1987), 48–49.
[105]Ibid., 26–27.

who had obvious administrative skills—could die without providing for his family and without anyone knowing why, even in rural Canada at the turn of the last century. Yet this was the reality that people in that time and place faced, even in the case of those who had strong natural skills.

Though his cause of death remains a mystery, we can speculate about why God allowed or caused Alexandre's death by examining the aftermath. It was, in many respects, a child's worse nightmare. Not only did they lose the love of their father, but they were all sent into abject poverty, living in a dilapidated one-room house. Every member of the family had to contribute to survive. Some worked odd jobs, some took care of the youngest siblings. Of particular help were the grown children of the first family, some of whom were almost as old as their stepmother. The older children, once they were married, would take in their younger siblings, thus lightening the load for their mother and stepmother while also adding a contributing member to their own household. The experience bonded the family together, especially to Andre, who was literally raised by all twenty surviving siblings and his mother, whom he adored. It also made all the family members resilient and industrious in a time when child labor was standard practice.

In the U.S. archives, I found an immigration card for my grandfather's brother Sylva from May 25, 1906, giving him clearance to move to Lewiston, Maine, from Beecher Falls, Vermont, a distance of over one hundred miles, to work as a shoemaker. He was twelve years old. Andre's first job at age twelve was to work as a cook's assistant at one of the lumber camps his father had previously managed. He was uncomfortable there, so he went to work at the Ethan Allen Furniture factory starting at age thirteen. As he put it, he looked old enough to fool the inspector and worked hard enough to satisfy the foreman. In 1919, now at the legal working age of sixteen, he moved to Berlin, New Hampshire, to work at the Brown Paper Company, living with his brother Mederic and his young family.

In 1921, Andre returned to Beecher Falls, Vermont, to be with his mother. He had saved $300, which was enough to buy a modest but pleasant two-story house for her. When he got home, they found he had pleurisy (fluid on the lungs) and had to have an incision between his ribs to drain the fluid. Later that year, he noticed a growth on his right leg, which a surgeon removed without anesthesia. In 1957, the doctors found bone cancer in the same leg, and this time they were forced to amputate it at the hip.

While his father's death was perplexing, it did form Andre into an industrious, compassionate young man, who was intensely family oriented. Knowing poverty and being on his own at such a young age taught him to be kind and accepting of all people, because he saw how little power he actually had over his own situation and was astute enough to know that others also lived through trials of their own. He used to tell me it was better to be lucky than good (meaning talented), because from his perspective, other people had easier lives than he did, despite his heroic efforts. I do not think he ever recognized how much more impressive his life work was compared to those lucky ones who never seemed to struggle.

If his character developed from the hardship of his father's death, his mother's death after a gallbladder operation on December 30, 1922, set in motion his adult life. Now parentless, and an adult in every sense, he needed to develop a purpose. Another tragedy provided an opportunity when his brother Sylva's wife, Rose, died unexpectedly, leaving him with three young daughters to raise. Hearing the news, Andre volunteered to help, moving to Lewiston, Maine. This was very much the family way, with younger siblings moving in with older siblings for mutual benefit.

He started working in a shoe shop but then, when he was laid off, worked at odd jobs.

The family was the center of social life as well for the French-Canadian immigrants in the area, many of whom were related by blood or marriage. They would have frequent family events, and at one of them, Andre met Adrian Gastonguay, who introduced him to his younger sister, Leona. Andre and Leona were married on July 5, 1926, at Sts. Peter and Paul Church in Lewiston, the largest church in Maine.

Looking solely from Andre's perspective, we can see how the deaths of both parents propelled his future state. The fact that he never knew his father was always troubling to him, as was the fact that no one could tell him how his father died. The little detail we think we know is that his father died unexpectedly at one of the lumber camps he managed, which were very rustic. Apparently, he drank some "bad water" and died, presumably from dysentery.

Andre equated all his suffering with bad luck. Looking at it a half century or more later, we can see how these experiences molded him. Andre felt abandoned by his father, so, not wanting anyone else to feel that pain, he embraced all members of his family for his entire life. He never lost ties with his siblings and their families and was loved by all of them. He was extremely paternal with his own children and grandchildren, making a huge effort to be present for them whenever needed. Every summer, he would call the extended family together for a lobster feast that he always paid for. Through his persistence and hard work in the face of immense hardship, he did for his children what his father had failed to do for him, enabling them through education and support to pursue their dreams.

When it was Andre's turn to die, in 1985, it was expected. He had been through terminal suffering and had been in a nursing home with dementia so severe that he no longer recognized even his wife, Marguerite, who as we already discussed, attended to him lovingly through it all. There was no mourning but more a celebration of a difficult life well lived. His funeral was attended by all of his direct descendants (twenty-three grandchildren and all of his five children and their spouses—except Claire, who predeceased him), and although all twenty-two of his siblings had predeceased him, someone from each of their families also attended, along with a number of friends and acquaintances. It was an awesome testament to how deep and broad his family connections were, and how much he loved and was loved. He was surely missed, but no one questioned why he died. He had completed his role in God's plan, and after a long and hard but inspiring life, he was called home. Although he never got the answer about how his father died, I think we understand at least in part that the reason was to propel Andre to fulfill the expectations he had of his father in his own life. There was undoubtedly more to it than that, because every life touches so many others and Alexandre had twenty-two other children, each with their own stories, but at least in Andre's case, the suffering did not break him—it refined him.

Chapter 20

Why Did My Spouse Die?

A good marriage is a true partnership, based on mutual love and respect, each partner willing to suffer for the good of the other. The good marriage is discreet, and it is fruitful, producing offspring that the couple shares in raising. The individual partners are not the same—they are complementary, filling each other's skill and resource gaps, each making the other better. When a person in a good marriage is dying, it puts pressure on both spouses. As the dying spouse loses capability, the other spouse is forced not only to pick up the tasks and responsibilities their dying spouse used to do—often because they were better suited to do so—but also to care for the dying spouse's accelerating health needs. This, coupled with the uncertainty of dying for one and the uncertainty of what it will mean to carry on alone for the other, can be overwhelming for both. If there are children involved, the stress ratchets up even further because their needs and fears for their futures must also be considered and dealt with.

My paternal grandfather, Andre Chaloux, married the love of his life, Leona Gastonguay, in 1926 at age twenty-three. They had six children together, although Roger, their first child, did not live beyond his first day. Unfortunately, in 1938, Leona contracted tuberculosis, which is highly contagious and required separation from the community. She was placed in a facility dedicated to tubercular care, the Maine State Sanatorium in Hebron, Maine, approximately fifteen miles from home. Andre could not care for her needs, work, and tend to his five young children, so he made the heartbreaking decision to put his three sons in the nun-run, state-funded Healy Asylum for orphaned boys and his daughters in the similarly run Marcotte Home for Girls (Irene, the youngest, was cared for by a relative until she was old enough to enter the Marcotte Home). My father, the middle child, was six when he entered the orphanage, and he stayed there until he was thirteen, coming home on the weekends.

Tuberculosis is caused by an airborne pathogen that can now be cured with a six-month regimen of drugs and prevented by the BCG vaccine, which was developed in France in 1921 and is required by law in most countries. This program was instituted in the United States in the 1950s but discontinued in 2005 when the CDC judged the side effects more dangerous than the chance of getting tuberculosis warranted.[106] Prior to the widespread use of the vaccine, tuberculosis was a feared public health concern that motivated the Maine state legislature to create the Maine State Sanatorium for Pulmonary Diseases in 1901. Lacking modern drug therapies, these sanatoriums sought to build up the patients' immune systems through careful management of their activities and environment. As it said in one of its pamphlets:

[106] Darcy Jiminez, "BCG: The History and Modern-Day Uses of the Tuberculosis Vaccine," October 4, 2010, https://www.pharma-ceutical-technology.com/features/bcg-vaccine-history-modern-uses-tuberculosis/.

In the treatment of tuberculosis, there are three considerations, Hygienic, Climatic, Dietetic, and a fourth, which is a combination of them all, Sanatorium treatment. This treatment means placing a patient under such health conditions as to strengthen his forces of life, and his resisting powers to the disease. It teaches him how to care for himself, the food and drink he is to take, and the time of taking. It regulates the hours to be spent out of doors, the amount of sleep, or time spent in bed, the things to do and the things not to do. It teaches him when and how to exercise, it means instruction in ventilation, clothing, the care of excretions and sputum, and it is just as important that these rules be carried out as it is for him to take his medicine. The carrying out of these rules, however, in the average home is almost impossible, for the patient is very apt to forget or become careless, and do things that may put him back for weeks or cause his death.[107]

In the first four years Leona was in the sanatorium, Andre visited as often as he could, but he did not own a car and so had to borrow a car from a relative. This was very stressful, no doubt, because he had to balance this with getting jobs to make money to pay the bills. Leona, unsurprisingly, preferred to live at home, so when she seemed to be recovering, Andre would bring her home. Inevitably, she would relapse and have to go to the local hospital, which would subsequently send her back

[107] "The Maine State Sanatorium for Pulmonary Diseases: Greenwood Mountain, Hebron, Maine, Incorporated 1901," DigitalCommons@UMaine, University of Maine, 23, https://digitalcommons. library.umaine.edu/cgi/viewcontent.cgi?article=1353&context =mainehistory.

to the sanatorium, only to start the process all over again. This went on for seven years.

World War II ironically was a godsend for Andre because he was able to get high-paying, steady employment building ships at the shipyard in Portland. This gave him the funds to buy his first car in 1942, which made his commute to Hebron much easier and more reliable than when he had to rely on friends and family to lend him their cars. Gas was rationed during the war, but Andre was able to negotiate for increased rations so that he could run a side business, charging co-workers for rides to and from the shipyard. He also bought his first house at 52 Sabattus Street in Lewiston, which would be his home for the next forty years.

For the following three years, Andre commuted thirty-six miles to work building ships at the Portland shipyard until his shift ended, then drove back to drop off his riders, then drove fifteen miles to Hebron to visit Leona in the hospital until the end of visiting hours and then fifteen miles back home to Lewiston. On the weekends, Andre would collect the children from the orphanages and, if Leona was feeling up to it, bring the family to see her. It was a grueling schedule to keep, and it weighed heavily on him. In 1945, Leona took a turn for the worse. Sensing that she was not improving at the sanatorium, Andre made the decision to bring her home for good. Marcel, 17, and Claire, 15, now old enough to care for themselves, were already living with their father, so they could also help provide care for their mother.

Leona's death on June 15, 1945, was traumatic. It happened in the early afternoon when Andre was away at work and Marcel, the oldest child, was at high school, helping pack up the chairs for the summer because it was the last day of school. Claire was responsible for her mother's care that day, and when Leona began coughing up copious amounts of blood, she was understandably unnerved and called her aunt, Leona's sister Aline. Aline came to the house — how she got there is unclear — and called the doctor, the shipyard, and the high school to let everyone know Leona had taken a turn for the worse. Marcel remembers being told he was urgently needed at home and sprinting home only to be too late. He recalls the scene being worse than he had imagined on the run home: his mother lay dead, surrounded by her own blood, and everyone was unsurprisingly upset, with no one knowing quite what to do.

Having just turned thirteen, my father remembered witnessing the event and described it much the same way, but Marcel does not remember him being there at that time. It was certainly a disconcerting scene for all of them, especially with the sobs of the heartbroken Andre when he arrived after what must have seemed like a very long thirty-six-mile drive at very high speeds — only to find out he had missed his beloved Leona's last breath by minutes. They had been married nineteen years, but Leona had been ill for seven of them.

Leona had suffered long enough, as had her family with her, particularly Andre, but also all of her children, who watched the trials of their parents as part-time orphans and, in the older children's cases, as caregivers. Having been through so much, they were all unsure about what the future would bring. Though people are often hesitant to acknowledge it, there is a feeling of relief when someone we are giving care to passes on, particularly if they have been suffering severely. This relief is for the deceased, who no longer suffers, but it is also for those of us who have been suffering right alongside them, both in the extra work and in the pain of watching a loved one suffer. If we become accustomed to caring for someone, we will also feel the loss of that responsibility as a void until we find something else to fill the time.

Dying without Fear

Immediately after the funeral, Andre made the first of a series of decisions that took the sting out of Leona's death for him as well as the children: he retrieved the remaining two children from the orphanages, so they were all reunited at home for the first time in seven years. This move did a lot for the anxiety of the children, since young people naturally worry about who will care for them when they lose a parent. When they were placed in the orphanage, the children had already effectively lost both parents, so Leona's death brought them back their father. They were together, but there were more challenges before they completely recovered.

As the war ended, so did Andre's employment at the shipyard. The year 1946 was a rocky one for the family. Though Andre worked odd jobs to feed his brood, it was not enough. The children were asked to find ways to make money, and when they did, they gave it all to their father to put in the general family fund. If they needed money for a date, they would make a request. They all knew enough about their living situation that they were always responsible about it, so there were no issues and none of them felt the situation was a hardship.

Good marriages last for the life of one of the spouses. When one partner dies, the other is free to marry again, but there will always be the first marriage that both a new spouse and the widow or widower will need to recognize and honor, particularly if the first union produced children, who naturally mourn the loss of their deceased parent and will reject anyone who challenges that memory or who changes the family dynamics.

By 1947, things had begun to turn around as Andre took some big steps. First, he married Marguerite Rancourt, who was thirty-eight at the time and had never married. She was part of Andre and Leona's social circle, so she was very aware of how strongly Andre loved Leona, but that did not deter her. Being naturally humble, she never sought to replace Leona; thus, once she and Andre were married, she asked Leona's children to call her by her first name instead of insisting that they address her with the word *Mother* or another familial term of endearment. She also kept a picture of Leona on the living room wall, close to where she died. Years later, when there were grandchildren, she repeatedly told us she was not our real grandmother, telling us about Leona. That made us love her all the more, and at her funeral, my cousin Karen, who gave the eulogy, spoke for all twenty-three of the grandchildren in confirming that she was not just a real grandmother but a great one.

In fact, she was the model second wife of a widower. She made a broken family whole again, not by trying to replace Leona as their mother but by simply seeking acceptance as a loving person whose goal was to share in their lives and do whatever she could to help out. Even with all that, she faced resentment from some of the children, and it took a while for her to be fully accepted. Marguerite told me that when she got married, she hoped it would last as long as Andre's first marriage of nineteen years. It actually lasted exactly twice as long (thirty-eight years) and ended with her immensely loving care of Andre as he was dying of dementia. I am certain that when they met in Heaven, Leona was very appreciative of how well Marguerite had cared for her family, making it her own without erasing Leona from the picture.

Because she had a steady job at the shoe factory, Marguerite was able to feed the family, freeing Andre and his three sons to add six apartments, and later a barbershop and beauty parlor, onto their home on 52 Sabattus Street, setting up a steady flow of income for the rest of his life. He later bought three more apartment buildings and, in 1965, converted his barbershop to a coin-operated laundromat, which he maintained. All three sons subsequently went to college and became successful engineers. As it turned out, their mother's death did not hold them back, but was in fact the springboard that allowed them all to ultimately flourish.

Despite all of that, there is still the question of why Leona had to have tuberculosis to begin with, why she needed to succumb to the health condition that caused all this suffering for the whole family. We cannot adequately answer this question based only on the human suffering her disease caused for the family but must also consider the spiritual growth that it engendered. By all accounts, Leona was a woman of strong faith, and she would have understood the concept of redemptive suffering. Because she suffered so much, she drew the whole family into sharing it with her. They all went through the four tasks of suffering, learning proper self-love, aligning themselves with God, loving their neighbors, and they all learned to sacrifice their own needs for the benefit of others, the highest form of love. She encouraged their persistence in the Faith by her own example. Because she was in the hospital, the children were educated by nuns in Catholic institutions. My father was very devout growing up because of that, as were his siblings.

Additionally, Marguerite got the family she wanted but never thought she would have, and she perfectly met the needs of our family. Andre lost his first love but gained a second one, who cared for him for close to forty years. Further, because he learned and pressed on despite a very challenging life, he died a successful businessman with many friends and a large, loving family that, through his efforts, was never impoverished again. If Leona was worried about the state of her family after her passing, she did not need to be—God's plan kept them whole because of her witness, not despite it.

One of the lessons of this story is that when your spouse is dying, all of their previous responsibilities will fall to you, along with their care. This can be overwhelming, as it was for my grandfather.

He turned to the Church for help, and Catholic institutions made it manageable for him by caring for his children for free for seven years. He turned to God when his life was in shambles, and the Lord solved all his problems. Perhaps that was why Leona had to die, to drive Andre and the whole family to depend on God. I am fairly certain that despite all his suffering, despite dying of dementia, he was very happy with how it all turned out, for him and for the family as well.

There are many other worthwhile lessons in this story. One is that we should trust in God's mercy and recognize that He can take hardship and make good come of it. Often, suffering helps us learn invaluable lessons that can benefit multiple generations. Finally, we should be content to be who we are and not try to be someone else. Marguerite did this to perfection, and she was loved because of it. If she had tried to replace Leona, she would have been resented by all those who had previously loved Andre's first wife.

My mother's experience with the death of my father was quite different. In October 2007, my father, Paul, had a stroke that left him with aphasia, which meant he could no longer read and he could no longer drive. This made him dependent on my mother to drive him, and she did not like to drive. My mother was also having her own medical problems, so my brother Richard, who never married, selflessly moved back in with them to lend a hand when needed. In late October 2011, my father had a second stroke, which proved to be fatal. As discussed previously, his doctor had terminally sedated him, so we knew approximately when he would die, and the family set up a vigil. As he passed, his children, now all adults, were around him, reading his biography, reminding him of all the good times we had shared.

My mother, always an emotional person, chose not to be there at the end. When he did pass on, I went to her house (where I was staying) and told her that my father had passed. I expected her to be distraught, so when she responded, "Thank God!" I was shocked. Then she told me that we had to let him go because he had suffered enough and was ready. She concluded that he would not want to live like that. The wisdom of what she said was lost on me at the time, but I understand now. As I wrote this, I realized for the first time that she had loved him so much that she was willing to let him go. Only after the funeral did she start thinking about herself and what she would do next. That problem actually had been pre-solved because my youngest sister, Maria, had a lot of space in her house and was eager to have her move in with her.

Chapter 21

Coping with Parental
Death as an Adult

Often, when our parents die in old age, there is nothing to mourn except the loss of their company. If they have led a good, full life ending with terminal suffering, then we need to do as my mother advised and let them go. In fact, if they die a good death, having reconciled with God, left no one in distress, and provided well for those they leave behind, then we should be happy for them as they graduate to eternal life. There should be no asking about why they died, because the answer is so obvious: it was their time to come home to the glory of the Lord.

If we have a hard time accepting this, we need to look at our own motivations. Perhaps we have become too dependent on our parents and need to become more independent. This is not to say that it is wrong to miss them—that is natural and right. But we can miss their presence and still be happy for them, loving them enough to let them go. And if we mourn for ourselves, it is time to take action to heed our suffering and obtain the goods we lack.

My mother's death was perfectly understandable. She was ninety years old and had been undergoing end-of-life suffering for months. Her dementia had reached the point that she could not move any of her limbs, and she could not eat or drink because she could no longer swallow. When the hospice nurse told us our mother had less than seventy-two hours to live, she was merely confirming what we already knew: her body had given out after ninety years, she had suffered enough, and God was calling her home.

Most parental deaths are understandable to adult children in much the same way. And most people in high-income countries die after terminal suffering in their seventies or older, as stated previously. So when our major organs give out or we get cancer, God calls us home, if we freely chose to enter the Kingdom and have learned to love as Jesus did. If the deceased is devout and loving, we can assume, with some plausibility, that God in His mercy has called the person home, either because he fulfilled his role or to protect him from future temptation to sin.

Chapter 22

Embracing Joy in Suffering and Death

There are two ways in which people approach terminal suffering and death. Those who do not know God will mistake suffering and death as punishment from an angry, vengeful Creator or will worry that God has abandoned them. Individuals with this frame of mind will exhibit anguish, self- absorption, and despair because there is no hope for anything better from a God they do not know and do not trust. These people follow their instincts, and two of our strongest instincts are to preserve our lives and to avoid suffering, which is really a transference of the instinct to avoid evil.

Without the good news about Jesus defeating death and inviting us to join Him in the Kingdom of God, we would be left with just our instinctual aversion to suffering and death. This is equivalent to trying to carry out the most important task of our existence without getting the directions or knowing the goal. It is understandable that a person in this situation would be frustrated and angry, but to direct those feelings toward God, who has been trying to get our attention through suffering and the evangelization efforts of the Church, is misguided and wrong.

If, on the other hand, we trust in God and the Church He left for us, then our mindset will be much different. We will understand that this world is just temporary, designed and built to give us the opportunity to experience the good that comes out of alignment with God and the suffering that results when we lack the required goods. We will understand that God is populating His Kingdom with those who are aligned with Him, with those who love all that is good, beautiful, and true, with those who are willing to suffer for the sake of His plan, taking up our crosses and following Him. We will also understand that what waits for us is the treasure of treasures—the Beatific Vision, our union with God. This means we will have access to His infinite imagination, which will satisfy our every desire, made even better by the opportunity to share it with all those who have learned to love completely and unconditionally, including, hopefully, those we have loved on earth.

Indeed, once we have the Catholic theology presented in the first section as a framework, approaching our own death takes on a very different feel than it does for most people. First of all, when we experience terminal suffering, we can see it as a blessing and not a curse. We can embrace it, no matter how painful, knowing that it will last only for a brief time in comparison to the eternity it is preparing us for and knowing that it is an indication of God's love for us that He has given us an unmistakable sign that we are about to die. This allows us to prepare for our meeting with Him face-to-face—and to prepare our survivors to carry on in a way that they, too, can partake of the divine nature and join in the utter happiness of being in the presence of God for eternity.

While others will lament their degradation and dependency, we can see these experiences as signs of the limitations of this life, as reminders of God's promise of better things in the life to come. We can be thankful for the motivation to seek out the higher things, rather than wasting all our time, energy, and resources on attaining material goods that will vanish with the existing world order on the Last Day (if they even last that long). We can also be comforted by the realization that our loved ones will suffer our loss less because we have had the opportunity to prepare them for it, both materially and spiritually. At the same time, we have confidence that we will be reunited with our loved ones in God's Kingdom for the rest of eternity.

For us, then, it is hard to see any reason for the anguish and self-absorption, the despair and revolt against God that others experience. Instead, we will find ourselves discerning what is important in life and what we should be doing in our remaining time on earth to reconcile with God and show our love for Him through our fidelity and our love of His children, our neighbors.

The great thing about all of this is God does not care how you began life; He cares about how you end life. If you are reading this book in the last moments of your life and you are moved to join the Creator in His Kingdom because you have developed a love of God, pray to Him with perfect contrition, and you can be saved, even if you led a horrible life.

And if any of you find this dubious or unfair, I direct you to the parable of the workers in the vineyard (Matt. 20:1–16). In this parable, a vineyard owner goes at dawn to hire workers for his vineyard. He hires a partial crew for the going daily wage and sends them to work. He goes out to the marketplace and hires more workers for the same wage at 9:00 a.m., noon, 3:00 p.m., and 5:00 p.m. At 6:00 p.m., the owner tells the foreman to pay the workers, starting with the ones who were hired last. They got the standard daily wage, so when the workers hired at dawn got the same wage, they were outraged. The owner told them, however, that they had not been cheated but had received exactly what they agreed on. He explained that as the owner he was free to be generous to the ones who came to work late. Just so, God has a special place in His heart for those who come to faith late in life. As Jesus said, "There will be more joy in heaven over one sinner who repents than over ninety-nine righteous people who have no need of repentance" (Luke 15:7).

This is completely consistent with the father of the Prodigal Son, who did not care that his son had lost his property—he just wanted his son back. God loves us so much that so long as we are sincerely willing to come back to Him, even if we wait until the hour of death, He wants us to join Him. This is certainly a cause for joy. But since we do not usually know the hour of our death, we should waste no time in getting prepared once we understand what God wants for and from us. Once we get in the state of grace, we just need to be diligent in aligning ourselves with God and, if we fail, going to Confession. At that point, having said yes to God's invitation, we can truly look forward to dying and death with joyous anticipation, no longer fearing them. By following Jesus, we will share in the divine nature and conquer death, living eternally in the presence of God, who fulfills our every need and desire.

Discussion Questions

Chapter 1

Have you ever felt called by God to
do something? What was it?

How did you know it came from God? Did you say yes?

What was the result of your choice,
and where did it lead you?

Chapter 2

How do you perceive God?

How did you come to your viewpoint?

Chapter 3

How has God shown love to you?

Chapter 4

Do you know of any examples where
good came from evil?

Chapter 5

Have you experienced any of the four
tasks of suffering? Explain.

Chapter 6

Have you been close to anyone with terminal suffering?

What was the experience like? How did they respond?

Chapter 7

Are you afraid of death? Why or why not?

What would the world be like if no one died?

Chapter 8

What do you imagine Heaven, Hell,
and Purgatory to be like?

What would you need to work on if
you ended up in Purgatory?

How do you think God would work on
that? Can you do that on earth?

Chapter 9

What are the implications of a new
heaven and a new earth?

Does this revelation help you with
concerns about suffering and death?

Chapter 10

How would you like to die? Why?

Chapter 11

What kind of care would you refuse even if
it would extend your life by five years?

What would you do with those extra five years?

Chapter 12

What would you do with your life if you were
given a diagnosis that gave you only six months
to live? If you were fully functional? If you were
in a wheelchair and in constant pain?

How would you create love, the only currency
that is good in Heaven and on Earth?

Chapter 13

Do you have a plan for yourself and your
survivors if you die unexpectedly?
If not, what can you do to fix this?

What would be your priorities?

Chapter 14

What would you do if you found out a
loved one committed suicide?

How can you help prevent that from happening?

Chapter 15

Has someone close to you died unexpectedly?
How did you cope with it?

What advice would you give others?

Chapter 16

If you become a caregiver, how would you
meet the five needs of your charge?

Chapter 17

When is it appropriate to turn over daily caregiving
to assisted living for a loved one or for yourself?

Chapter 18

Have you ever known an innocent child
who died? Was the child loved?

Was the family better off having had
the child, even for a brief time?

Chapter 19

Have you planned for your unexpected
death for your young children?

Have you talked to them about what
happens when you die?

Have you planned for their care and ongoing support?

Chapter 20

If you died next week, how prepared would
your spouse be to live his or her daily life?

Is there something you can do to make
your spouse's life easier just in case?

Would you have any regrets? What
can you do now to rectify this?

Chapter 21

If your parents are alive, will you mourn
their deaths or celebrate their lives?

If you do not feel their lives are worth celebrating,
are you judging them too harshly?

What good things have they done or are they
doing? Is there something you can do to help?

Chapter 22

Do you feel loved or abandoned by God? Why?

Can you see the possibility that your suffering
may be leading you home to God?

About the Author

Dr. Paul Chaloux teaches theology as an adjunct professor at the Catholic University of America and teaches a course on suffering at the Avila Institute for Spiritual Direction. He serves as a catechist at St. Agnes Parish in Arlington, Virginia. He has been married to his wife, Sue, for thirty-five years. They have four adult children and three granddaughters.

Sophia Institute

Sophia Institute is a nonprofit institution that seeks to nurture the spiritual, moral, and cultural life of souls and to spread the gospel of Christ in conformity with the authentic teachings of the Roman Catholic Church.

Sophia Institute Press fulfills this mission by offering translations, reprints, and new publications that afford readers a rich source of the enduring wisdom of mankind.

Sophia Institute also operates the popular online resource CatholicExchange.com. *Catholic Exchange* provides world news from a Catholic perspective as well as daily devotionals and articles that will help readers to grow in holiness and live a life consistent with the teachings of the Church.

In 2013, Sophia Institute launched Sophia Institute for Teachers to renew and rebuild Catholic culture through service to Catholic education. With the goal of nurturing the spiritual, moral, and cultural life of souls, and an abiding respect for the role and work of teachers, we strive to provide materials and programs that are at once enlightening to the mind and ennobling to the heart; faithful and complete, as well as useful and practical.

Sophia Institute gratefully recognizes the Solidarity Association for preserving and encouraging the growth of our apostolate over the course of many years. Without their generous and timely support, this book would not be in your hands.

www.SophiaInstitute.com
www.CatholicExchange.com
www.SophiaInstituteforTeachers.org

Sophia Institute Press is a registered trademark of Sophia Institute.
Sophia Institute is a tax-exempt institution as defined by the
Internal Revenue Code, Section 501(c)(3). Tax ID 22-2548708.